SAINTS

ADVENTURES IN COURAGE

SAINTS

ADVENTURES IN COURAGE

BY MARY O'NEILL
ILLUSTRATED BY ALEX ROSS

DOUBLEDAY & COMPANY, INC.
Garden City, New York

NIHIL OBSTAT
Daniel V. Flynn, J.C.D.
Censor Librorum

IMPRIMATUR
☩ Francis Cardinal Spellman
Archbishop of New York
May 8, 1963

The *nihil obstat* and *imprimatur* are official declarations
that a book or pamphlet is free of doctrinal or moral
error. No implication is contained therein that those
who have granted the *nihil obstat* and *imprimatur* agree
with the contents, opinions or statements expressed.

The stories about the saints in this book are drawn wherever possible from historic fact; included in a few of them
are beloved old Christian legends without which it would
be impossible to tell the story of the saint in question.

To a wonderful teacher,
SISTER IRMA DONAHUE, M.A., C.S.J.

CONTENTS

SAINTS

ADVENTURES IN COURAGE

SAINT ANNE

THE GRANDMOTHER OF JESUS

Saint Anne, the grandmother of Jesus, was born in Palestine more than two thousand years ago. Few little girls in those days ever went to school. Anne, the daughter of wise and wealthy parents, was one of the lucky ones. She attended the boarding school attached to the beautiful Jewish temple in Jerusalem, the capital city of Palestine.

Jerusalem was an exciting city in those days. Built on top of the highlands of Judea, it was ruled by the Romans. It was a great trade center, and the people, customs, costumes, and languages of Asia, Greece, Rome, Africa, Syria, and Egypt gave it the look of a great, never-ending carnival. Day and night colorful camel caravans carrying news, spices, gold, and precious stones filled the busy streets.

Here, in this thrilling city, Anne spent all her girlhood. She learned to love God dearly and all of His creation: the people, the hills and valleys, the sky, all flowers and animals, water and sunshine, the mountains and the stars. She learned to spin and sew, to cook and weave and garden, to sing the Psalms and memorize Scripture. Each day with her schoolmates and teachers she visted the temple. Her prayers were the prayers of all her people: she begged God to send the promised Redeemer soon, and to free the Jews from their Roman conquerors.

Before Anne's education was quite complete, her mother died. During her last illness Anne left school to be with her. She remained at home from then until her marriage, keeping house for her father. The death of her mother was Anne's first great sorrow.

But a new love was soon to come to her. The rich and handsome sheep owner, Joachim, wished to marry her. Knowing the goodness of Joachim, and their love for each other, Anne's father gave his consent, and a year later they became husband and wife. Joachim took his young bride to his home in Jerusalem, and for a while they were very happy.

But as the years went by the homes of their young married friends and relatives were filled with children. Anne and Joachim, who longed for a family, had none. They prayed constantly for a baby, but they were not given even one.

Among people in those days, a childless marriage was considered a punishment of God. Soon Anne and Joachim were laughed at and mocked because they had no family. This went on for many years and became a sorrow that clouded all their days.

But through all those years Anne and Joachim never questioned God's will. They kept on loving and trusting Him. And after twenty years of waiting their love and trust and prayers were all rewarded. Anne was going to have a baby at last!

And how well worth waiting for this one was! Angels leaned over this sweetest of all girl babies, smiling and singing the dear Scripture verse:

"Who is she, who comes up out of the desert, like a cloud of perfume, of myrrh and of incense? How beautiful you are, Beloved One, how beautiful you are, and filled with sweetness!"

Heaven and earth that day and forever would praise Anne and Joachim, for the little girl born to them was Mary, who would someday be the mother of Jesus, the Son of God, the Redeemer of the world.

SAINT JOSEPH

FOSTER FATHER OF JESUS AND
PATRON OF REFUGEES

Long, long ago in the little town of Nazareth in Palestine there lived a young carpenter named Joseph. He was poor, for although his work was fine, out of pity for those poorer than he was he charged little for it. And he was noble. Noble in all his ways, and a direct descendant of the Jewish King, David.

At twenty-five Joseph was still unmarried, still searching for a lovely young woman whose mind and body and spirit were perfection. And then one day in the temple at Jerusalem a high priest introduced him to Mary, the beautiful young daughter of Joachim, the sheep merchant. From the moment Joseph saw her, until the moment of his death, his desire was to cherish and protect her. Mary and Joseph became engaged.

In a dream Saint Joseph learned from an angel that Mary was to become the mother of Jesus, the Redeemer. And that this Child of God would be his Foster Son. Being a humble man with a deep love for his Creator, Joseph was stunned by this honor. On the Sabbath following this dream, Joseph and Mary were married. The high priest in the temple called down the blessing of the Lord upon them both.

Joseph and Mary lived in the little hilly town of Nazareth. The streets were narrow and winding. Donkeys pulled the market carts. Children played hopscotch on the roads, marking out the squares with their sandaled feet. Women carried water for their homes from deep wells.

Everyone in Nazareth lived in caves in those days. These caves were airy and pleasant. Each was cut out of the solid rock of the hillsides. The home of Joseph and Mary was larger than the others, for Joseph's carpenter shop was attached to it. Outside, between fig and olive trees, cut lumber was piled to season in the sun.

In his shop Joseph made tables, cupboards, doors, cradles, beds, and

chairs. And wonderful toys from wood scraps. His shop was always filled with shaving curls, sawdust, and building blocks. Everyone for miles around came to Joseph when they needed anything built of wood. He was a fine workman and a good friend.

Jesus met all of the men of Nazareth in Joseph's shop. But none of them ever pleased Him as much as His father. For Joseph was big and strong, patient and kind, and fun to be with. On rainy days all of Jesus' young friends played with Him in Joseph's carpenter shop.

Jesus must have loved trips into the hills with Joseph. There, they could cut down trees for building lumber. There they could eat their lunch of bread and cheese, figs and goat's milk, picnic-fashion on the grass. And there at work's end there must have been stories. Probably the most exciting one was the tale of the Flight into Egypt, told in Joseph's way:

"Your mother missed Nazareth when we were in Egypt. She was homesick. Just before You were born, Caesar, the Roman ruler, ordered a census of his empire. Each family had to go back to the town where their family began, and register their name at the court-house. We, of the house of David, had to go to Bethlehem. You were born there. We meant to come back to Nazareth as soon as Your mother was strong enough to travel. But King Herod changed our plans."

Can't you see Joseph pause in his story-telling to select a piece of new wood, draw out his knife, and begin to shape a toy in his hands?

"Three wise men came from far away to visit You. They stopped at Herod's court and asked where in Bethlehem they might find You. King Herod was jealous. Poor man, he thought You, a little baby, wanted *his* kingdom! And to be very sure You would not grow up and take his crown, he did a terrible thing. He ordered his soldiers to kill all Jewish boy children up to two years old living in or near Bethlehem. An angel warned me of this in a dream. I wakened and told Your mother. Then I lifted her onto our donkey and placed You in her arms. We fled into Egypt by the back roads. By morning You were safe from the murderous soldiers and we were in a strange land. Herod died a few months later. And in a dream again an angel told me that it was safe for us to return. Then we came home to Nazareth,

[19]

You and Your mother and I. It was good to be home and have a Little Boy in the house. All our friends and relatives came to welcome You. They thought You were a fine, strong, beautiful child. We had a grand feast. Now, we'd better gather up the wood and get on down the hill or Your mother will wonder what's become of us."

Evening was the best time of day. Work was over. Jesus, Mary, and Joseph were together in their home. Pretty soon little Jesus would get ready for bed. He would take with Him a new toy Joseph had carved for Him in the afternoon as they rested together on the hillside.

SAINT ANDREW

APOSTLE, PATRON OF RUSSIA AND SCOTLAND

Saint Andrew was the first of the apostles chosen by Jesus. He was the son of Jona, a fisherman of Bethsaida, in Galilee. Saint Peter was his brother.

One day when Andrew was walking in the countryside with Saint John the Baptist, Jesus passed by. Looking after Him, John turned toward Andrew and said: "Behold the Lamb of God!"

Saint Andrew understood by these words that he had just seen the Redeemer of the world. In those days little lambs were offered in the Jewish temple as a sign of love for God. This offering was called a sacrifice. In calling Jesus the Lamb of God, John meant that Jesus was the sacrifice God would make for our redemption. Thinking of this, Andrew ran after Him, caught up with Him, and they spent two hours together.

During this visit Andrew was convinced that Jesus was the long-promised Messiah. He showed his faith and love and joy, and it was then that Jesus chose him as the first apostle.

After that meeting Andrew rushed home to tell his family that he had met and talked with Jesus. He could hardly wait to take his brother, Simon, to meet Him. Jesus received them warmly, and changed Simon's name to Peter, and made him the second apostle. Shortly after this Andrew and Peter left their home and their fishing boats to follow Jesus wherever He went. They preached the new faith He had taught them and baptized in His name.

Historians tell us that Saint Andrew carried Christianity into Greece and Rome. There is a legend that he preached in Kiev, a city in the Ukraine province of Russia. And we know that he is the patron saint of Russia.

From tradition we learn that Saint Andrew was crucified at Patras in Achaia, a land which today would be part of western Greece. We

are told that he was bound, rather than nailed, to his cross, and that hanging from it he preached to those around him for two days before he died.

Old legends tell us that Saint Rule, a bishop of Patras, was warned by an angel in a dream to take the relics of Saint Andrew and to go "toward the ends of the earth" in a northwesterly direction until he was stopped by an angel.

Taking some of the relics of Saint Andrew, Saint Rule began his journey. It seemed an endless wandering by land and sea. After more than a year of travel without map or guide he was given a sign that his journey was now complete. He had arrived at the place that is now the city of Saint Andrews in Scotland. There he built a church to shelter the relics, and there he began to preach the faith of Jesus to the people of the land. The feast celebrating the arrival of the relics is still kept in the archdiocese of Saint Andrews in Scotland every May 9.

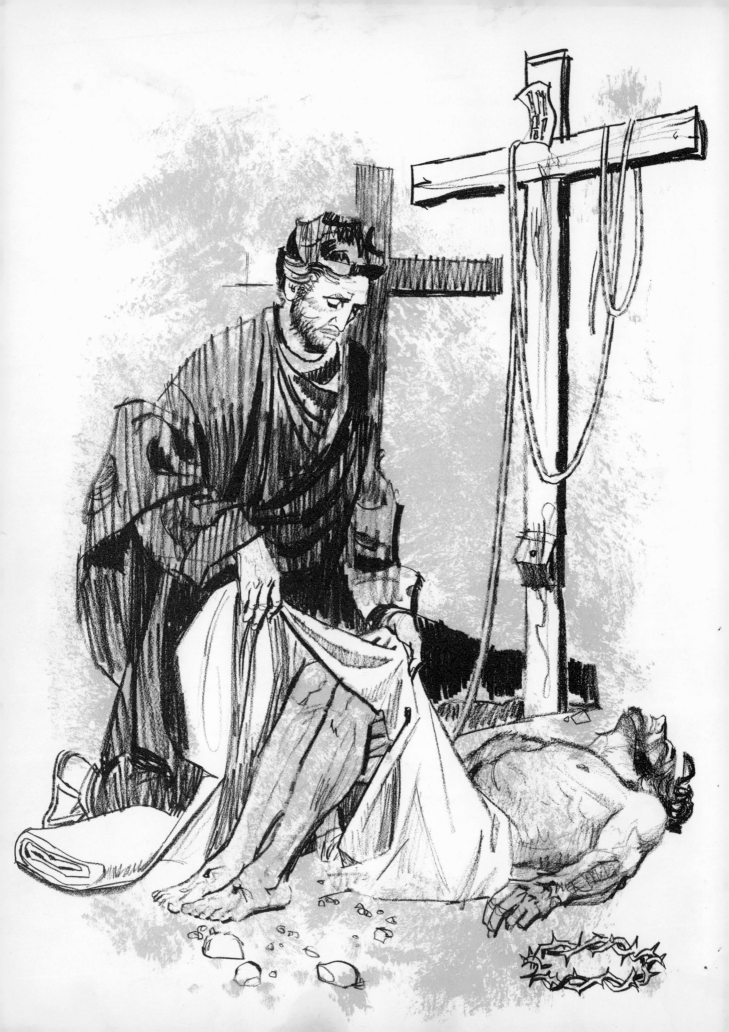

SAINT JOSEPH
OF ARIMATHEA
THE LAWYER

All that we know of Joseph of Arimathea happened to him in a few hours of one day in his lifetime. That day was the saddest one the world has ever known. It was the first Good Friday. And the hours were those while Christ was dying on the Cross, and immediately after His dead body was taken down.

The one brave, loving act of Joseph on this day is told to us in the Gospels of Matthew, Mark, Luke, and John, as it will be told to others centuries from now.

Joseph of Arimathea was a secret disciple of Jesus. He wasn't one of the courageous ones who followed Him openly. He was a lawyer. Perhaps he was afraid people would not bring their cases to him if they knew he believed in the new religion of Jesus. We know he was a good and just man, and that he did not take any part in the vote that condemned Jesus. We will never know for certain why he was afraid to be known as a Christian. But we do know that all fear left him on the day Christ died on the Cross. For it was Joseph of Arimathea who went boldly to Pilate, the Roman Governor, and begged for the body of Jesus. His request was granted, and when Christ was removed from the Cross, His wounded body was given to Joseph for burial. Joseph wrapped it tenderly in fine linen and placed it in his own fine new Sepulcher which was hewed out of rock, and in which no man had ever before been laid.

With this act Joseph openly declared himself a Christian, and accepted all that might happen to him, to his business and his family. He did this at the time when the faith of many faltered because their Leader was dead.

This is all we know about Joseph of Armithea, one of the first Christian saints.

[25]

SAINT JOHN
THE BELOVED DISCIPLE

Saint John is called "the disciple whom Jesus loved." He is also known as Saint John the Divine and Saint John the Evangelist.

Saint John was the son of a fisherman called Zebedee and his wife, Salome. He grew up with his parents and his older brother, James, alongside the Sea of Galilee in Palestine. He and his brother became fishermen, too.

This was "Christ's country", the land in which He lived, and the place from which He began His public life. It was here that He met James and John and chose them as two of His apostles.

Saint John was one of the most honored men who ever lived, for during the last three years of Christ's life on earth John was His friend, as loved and as familiar as a young brother. John learned his Christian faith from the lips of Jesus, Himself. He was with Him when crowds gathered to praise Him. He was with Him when He worked miracles. And he was with Him all that long three lonely hours when He was dying on the Cross.

And it was while Jesus was dying that He looked down upon His mother and John and said: "Woman, behold thy son."

And to John: "Behold thy mother."

And from that hour until her death, Saint John cared for Mary as if she were his mother. And she regarded him as her son.

After the death of our Lord, Saint John and Saint Peter were imprisoned for teaching Christian doctrine. When they were released, Saint John remained in Jerusalem, preaching with Saint Peter and Saint James. In this city the apostles converted thousands, held the Council of Jerusalem, and planned their missions. John left Palestine to carry the new faith into Asia Minor and made his home in the city of Ephesus. In his middle years he traveled constantly as a missionary. Because of the great, hopeful message he carried, and the gentle manner in which he delivered it, he was dearly loved by the people. The teachings of Jesus spread rapidly through Asia Minor. As John grew older he turned his mission tasks over to younger priests, and began the work which was to make him famous throughout the Christian world. He began to write the thrilling Gospel according to Saint John, three Epistles, and a book of prophecy called the Apocalypse.

When Saint John was a very old man and could no longer preach long and glorious sermons to the people, he was carried to them. Looking out over the sea of upturned faces, and scarcely able to speak, he reduced Christ's noble message to six words: "My little children, love one another." And when he was asked why he always preached this same little sermon, he said: "Because it is the word of the Lord, and if you keep it you do enough."

Saint John lived to see the second century, and died in Ephesus. This once important city exists no more. But the land that held it is often pointed out to visitors today in modern Turkey.

SAINT MARY MAGDALEN

THE FRIEND OF JESUS

The Sea of Galilee is in the State of Israel, now. When Israel was still Palestine, there was a lovely little seaside town on its western shore. It was called Magdala. The town is gone now. No one would ever remember it at all were it not for one person who once lived there. It was the home of Mary Magdalen.

Mary Magdalen was very beautiful. She had always been beautiful. Her eyes were the color of fresh violets. Her lips were soft and pink as wild roses. Her hair was long and it flowed like a veil of golden gossamer around her. She was tall and graceful as a willow tree. And she was vain. All her thoughts were centered around herself and the worldly things that comforted her appetite and kept her so envied and so attractive. People said she was a very wicked woman, and a trouble-maker. And perhaps at one time she was.

Mary Magdalen's beauty hadn't brought her much happiness. She was lonely inside it. She was watched and talked-about all the time. Most people avoided her. Few had a kind word to say about her.

One afternoon while she was out walking, she saw that a crowd had gathered in Galilee. Being curious, she stopped to see what was going on. She was wearing her lovely silks and jewels, and they rustled and tinkled as she walked. People turned to look at her. They always did. And they saw that, as usual, she was carrying her little alabaster box.

She was never without this precious box. It held her rouge and lipstick, eyebrow pencil and perfume. And spikenard from India. Spikenard was a most costly oil. It was used to smooth and scent the skin. Only the very richest people could afford it.

As Mary stood on the edge of the crowd she heard Jesus speaking. She had never heard or seen anyone like Him before. His words thrilled and comforted her. He seemed to be speaking directly to her. She forgot herself, and listened to the end. What an idea for living He had, she thought! It was lovely. And she wanted to know more about it.

When Jesus had finished speaking a rich man in the crowd asked Him to dinner. Mary Magdalen followed them to the man's house. It was the custom in those days to greet guests in the home with a kiss, to remove their sandals and wash their feet in cool water and to dry them with a fresh linen towel. The man who invited Jesus did not bother to do this. Seeing this carelessness she was moved with a feeling of compassion so new to her that she could not control it.

When they were seated at table, Mary Magdalen rushed into the dining room. She fell, weeping, at the feet of Jesus. She washed His tired feet with her tears. She wiped them with her golden, fine-spun hair. And then she opened her alabaster box. She poured the precious spikenard, soft and scented, upon His sacred feet. And then she kissed them.

Seeing this, the rich man told Jesus laughingly that she was a great sinner. But He did not turn her away. Instead, He said to the man: "Many sins are forgiven her, because she hath loved much."

And bending to Mary, He said: "Thy sins are forgiven thee. Thy faith hath made thee safe. Go in peace."

Mary felt clean and new as springtime. Goodness bloomed like an exciting flower in her heart. She hated her old, vain ways. She tossed them away, forever.

Jesus knew what had happened inside her heart. And once again He said of her: "Amen, I say to you—wheresoever this Gospel shall be preached in the whole world, that also which she hath done shall be told for a memorial of her."

Years later we hear from Saint John Chrysostom: "And behold! what He said has come to pass. Wherever you go you will hear her praises sung.... The dwellers in Persia, in India... in the British isles celebrate this deed."

In the darkest hour of Jesus' life, as He lay dying on the cross, she was there. Bearing sweet spices and weeping before His tomb, she was the first to see Him rise gloriously from the dead.

Beautiful and radiant as God, He called her name: "Mary!"

As she turned and saw Him that first Easter morning, she cried out: "Master!" The story of Mary Magdalen is one of the sweetest and most hopeful in Holy Scripture.

SAINT PAUL

APOSTLE OF THE GENTILES

You probably know a boy like Saul. Smart and cocky. Small for his age, wiry and strong. Able to say things well, and in a few words. A good friend and a bitter enemy. Stubborn. Fond of his own way. And lovable.

Schooldays were long in Tarsus, the town in which Saul lived. After lessons in reading, writing, and arithmetic, trade school began. Every boy in Tarsus had to learn a trade. Saul became a tent maker. He was a very good one.

Today, Tarsus is a little town in southwest Turkey. When Saul lived there in the first century A.D. it was an important city in Cilicia in Asia Minor.

One day his father said to him: "We are proud of you, Saul. We are sending you to Jerusalem to study the law and the scriptures under the great teacher, Gamaliel."

It was in Jerusalem that Saul first heard the name of Jesus. This is what his friends were saying: "Jesus said He was the Son of God! Imagine that! He even called Himself the Messiah! The blasphemer! We must get rid of His followers. Since His death they grow in numbers everywhere."

Soon young Saul began to hate all those who followed Jesus. Impatient with those who talked against Him but failed to act, Saul decided to crush the Christians himself. Hearing that there were many in the city of Damascus, he gathered a band of soldiers together and rode off to arrest them.

[32]

The road to Damascus, in Syria, dips through a valley of great beauty. But Saul saw none of it. In a frenzy of hatred, he pushed forward, thinking only of the punishments he would inflict on the Christians he captured and the glory he would gain for his bravery. He would not allow his men to rest even a minute in the cool, green valley shade.

Pushing, sweating, lashing their weary horses, Saul and his soldiers neared the gates of Damascus. Suddenly a blinding flash of light struck down like a sword from the sky and knocked Saul from his horse. He fell to the ground and did not move. The bright, unearthly light surrounded him. The air whirred with frightening sound. Soldiers trembled and their horses reared and plunged in terror. Then a clear Voice from above cried out:

"Saul, Saul, why dost thou persecute Me?"

"Who art Thou, Lord?" Saul whispered, weakly.

"I am Jesus, whom thou dost persecute," the Voice answered.

"Lord what wilt Thou have me do?" Saul asked.

"Arise, and go into the city, and there it shall be told thee what thou must do," said the Voice.

Saul rose from the ground. With dusty hands he rubbed his eyes. He was blind! Proud Saul with bent head was led fumbling by his troubled soldiers into the house of Judas on Strait Street in Damascus.

Three days later Jesus appeared to Ananias, a Christian, and said: "Arise, and go into the street that is called Strait and seek, in the house of Judas, one named Saul of Tarsus; for, behold, he prayeth."

Ananias was afraid of Saul. He said: "Lord, I have heard from many of this man, how great evils he hath done to Thy saints in Jerusalem."

But our Lord answered him: "Go; for this man is a vessel of election to me, to carry my name before the Gentiles and kings, and the children of Israel."

Ananias obeyed, for his love for Jesus was greater than his fear. He found Saul and comforted him. He touched his eyes gently and when Saul opened them he could see. He led him into the lovely, quiet garden outside Judas's home, and there, according to Saul's wishes, he baptized him, and gave him a new name, Paul.

Saul, who had hated Christians, was now Paul, who loved everyone. All the rest of his life was one long journey for Jesus. He carried His teachings into all the countries between the Black Sea and the Mediterranean. He wrote long letters to those new Christians he left behind, to advise them and strengthen their faith. These letters are called the Epistles of Saint Paul. They are a precious part of the Bible.

Paul was arrested and imprisoned for his faith many times: in Philippi, in Jerusalem, in Caesarea, and in Rome. And finally, in Rome he was beheaded for it. Strong and brave, he who had once hated Jesus was happy to give his life for Him.

Under sentence of death in a Roman prison, Paul wrote a farewell letter to his dear friend, Saint Timothy, Bishop of Ephesus in Asia Minor. The words are those of a soldier: "I am even now ready to be sacrificed, and the time of my dissolution is at hand. I have fought a good fight. I have finished my course. I have kept faith. As for the rest, there is laid up for me a crown of justice which the Lord, the just judge, will render to me in that day: and not only to me, but to them also that love His coming."

SAINT PETER

PRINCE OF THE APOSTLES

When Christ was a young man, Galilee and the fresh-water Sea of Galilee within it were part of Palestine and under Roman rule.

The gentle hills sloping down to the sea gave farmers a rich harvest of dates, figs, olives, and pomegranates. The scent of fruit and the sea view made people want to walk slowly through this lovely country. Below the hills lay the sparkling sea filled with delicious fish. Along its shores lived the fishermen. Here, on a clear morning you could see them beach their boats, unload their catch, mend their nets, and spread them across warm sands to dry.

This was the country in which Christ spent His childhood. And, as a young man, it was to these people that He preached.

In the town of Bethsaida lived Simon, one of the best fishermen in Galilee. He was a gruff, bossy, outspoken man but known to have a kind and generous heart. People in his neighborhood looked to him for advice and leadership.

When Simon first heard Christ his big heart filled with love and admiration. He believed this gentle man was the Son of God, and loudly, before a listening crowd, he said so. It was then that the young Jesus gave this bold and sturdy fisherman the name of Peter, which means "rock."

Peter had many faults. He often changed his mind. Many times he spoke without thinking and said things which he was sorry for later. He was often boastful.

God understood and loved Peter and made him one of His twelve apostles.

[37]

Peter followed Christ as he went from place to place, preaching and working miracles. It was Peter who tried to protect Him from the crowds, who worried about food and lodging for Him, and who constantly sought little comforts for his Master.

God, who knows us better than we know ourselves, knows that often, when our friends are in serious trouble and need us, we are sometimes too frightened and ashamed to say that we even know them. Bold, loving Peter said he would never deny his Master. He swore that though the whole world desert Him, He could count on Peter to remain faithful. But, when Jesus asked him to watch and pray with Him during the Agony in the Garden of Gethsemane, poor Peter fell asleep! And when Jesus was being condemned to death, Peter was asked three times if he knew Christ and, frightened, three times he said he did not know Him! He who wished to appear always strongest in Jesus' eyes, many times, like all of us, appeared weak and foolish. But Peter's love for God was greater than all his failures. Jesus knew how deep that love was when He said to him: "Thou art Peter; and upon this rock I will build my church and the gates of hell shall not prevail against it. And I will give to thee the keys of the Kingdom of Heaven. . . ."

Peter spread the teachings of his Master far and wide. He was the first Pope. And for him is named the Church of St. Peter's in Rome, the capital church of Christianity. Saint Peter wrote two short Epistles, or letters, to his followers. The first one contains five chapters, and was written in Rome, fifteen years after Christ's death. In it Saint Peter instructs all Christians with the dignity and authority of the Prince of the Apostles. The second Epistle contains only three chapters. This was written thirty-five years after Jesus' death, and just before Peter's own martyrdom. In it he reminds us of our great gifts from God, warns against false teachers, and describes the end of the world and the day of judgment.

Saint Peter, like Christ, was crucified. But he felt he was unworthy to die upon a cross with his head facing Heaven, as Christ had done. He asked to be placed head downward on his cross. And this was done.

SAINT MOSES
THE STRONG MAN

Moses was a huge, fierce Ethiopian giant, and a slave in the house of an Egyptian official. He was dismissed from his master's house after repeated thefts and much misconduct. Angered, he gathered a group of bandits around him and terrorized the countryside.

One day while he was walking alone he became hungry and decided to steal a lamb and roast it. But the dog in charge of the fold barked so loudly Moses had to flee without his lamb. Now he was not only still hungry, but angry as well, and he swore he would kill the shepherd of this flock. To get at him he had to swim across the River Nile with his sword in his teeth. The shepherd, who was afraid of him, hid in a sand cave and Moses could not find him. Furious, he gave up his search, killed four rams, tied them together, and towed them back across the river. He butchered them, cooked and ate the meat, sold their hides for wineskins, and walked fifty miles to join his gang. That was the sort of man Moses was.

Moses now drops out of sight and we hear no more of him for a while. But it is thought that after other evil-doing he hid from the police in a monastery of the desert monks of Egypt and that his heart was touched by their peaceful, honest life. Perhaps it was there that he first heard of the teachings of Jesus, the kind and loving Master. For the next we hear of Moses he has given up his life of banditry and is living in a monk's cell at the monastery of Petra in the desert of Skete in Egypt. Here, he was attacked in his cell by four robbers. With his great strength he overpowered them, tied them together, slung them across his back and carried them into the monastery church. There he dumped them on the floor, saying to the astonished monks: "I am not allowed to hurt anybody, so what do you want me to do with these?" It is said these robbers later became monks themselves.

Moses did not conquer himself in a day. The old, familiar urge to

violence did not die easily or quickly within him. Discouraged because his improvement seemed so slow, he consulted the abbot at Petra. The abbot took him to the roof of a house just before dawn: "See," he said, "the light only *gradually* drives away the darkness. So it is with the soul."

Through all discouragement his deep love of God never waned. Finally, by work, fasting, prayer, and study, Moses the former bandit was ordained a priest by Theophilus, Archbishop of Alexandria, Egypt. He was an example of devotion to all who knew him.

When a raid by the wild Berber tribesmen threatened his desert monastery, Moses refused to allow his monks to defend themselves. He made them run away before it was too late, telling them: "All that take the sword shall perish with the sword."

He remained, and with seven who would not leave him, he was killed in the Berber raid. Moses was seventy-five years old then. He was buried in the monastery called Dair al Baramus, which still stands in Egypt.

[41]

SAINT JUSTIN
MARTYR

Saint Justin was born in the second century at Flavia Neapolis, on the northeast shore of the Aegean Sea. His parents were well-educated, wealthy Greeks. And they were pagans. When Justin was a little boy his teachers said that someday he would be a great scholar. And they were right. School days were never long enough for him.

In those days schooling was over for most young men when they had completed courses in history, poetry, grammar, reading, and arithmetic. Only a few went on to higher learning. Justin was one of the few. He wanted to know what people believed, how and why their beliefs affected their conduct.

There were many religions at that time, and Justin studied all the popular ones. When his difficult studies were over he was given a special cloak to wear. It was called a philosopher's cloak. Because only a few men ever won the right to wear this garment they were instantly recognized and honored wherever they went.

One day when Justin was about thirty years old he was walking along the seashore with his cloak across his shoulders. He felt restless and discouraged. With all his knowledge he had not yet found a faith in which he, himself, could believe. He met an old man, and they began to talk. The old man told him about a way of life he had found that brought happiness and hope to heart and mind. He was so convincing that Justin began at once to study this faith, which was called Christianity. Everything about it delighted him. He became a Christian.

Up to this time there had been very few among the persecuted early Christians who were able to express themselves in writing, preaching, and debate as well as Justin. He felt there were many thousands who would accept the teachings of Jesus gladly, if they were clearly explained. And he was right. Instead of hiding in fright he went about boldly in his cloak preaching and writing about Christianity. He was particularly successful in making converts among the well educated in Ephesus in Asia Minor, in Alexandria in Egypt, and in Rome.

Marcus Aurelius, the Roman Emperor, ruled from 161 to 180. His reign was marked by bitter persecution of the Christians. Justin knew this when he went to Rome the first time. While there he made many converts, among them a group of Roman aristocrats and scholars. When word of this reached the pagan rulers of the city they swore to take him prisoner the next time he entered Rome. It was easy to recognize him in his philosopher's cloak, and he made no attempt to hide. He was arrested, accused of being a Christian, and brought before the Roman prefect, Rusticus. He made a bold confession of his love and belief in the truth of the teachings of Jesus. Scornfully he refused to bow before the pagan gods. With six of his followers he was condemned to die. They were all beheaded with him in Rome, in the year of our Lord, 165.

The acts of Saint Justin's trial and martyrdom are among the most valuable and accurate which have come down to us from early Christian times.

SAINT VALENTINE

THE PATRON OF LOVERS

In the year 270, Claudius the Second, Emperor of Rome, issued a law which he hoped would rid the empire of Christians. He ordered his spies and soldiers, under threat of punishment, to find Christians wherever they were, to arrest them, and bring them before the judges. Then, if they refused to worship idols, they would be sentenced to death.

The Christians knew how they would die if they were caught. They would be thrown to lions, beheaded, or crucified. Not wishing to give up their faith, or to die, they went into hiding and practiced their religion secretly. But the soldiers gave them no rest. Their hiding places were discovered. They were arrested. They refused to offer homage to the idols. They were condemned to death. The Roman jail was full of them.

The legend of Saint Valentine is built around his love and care of those who were condemned to death for their faith.

Valentine was a young Roman noble and a priest. He was safe from arrest, for he was not even suspected of being a Christian. And he had work to do among other Christians like himself. He knew that if he were seen consoling these prisoners he would be arrested and accused of being one of them. Nevertheless he felt that it would not be too risky to visit them once. So, filling his pockets with little treats, he went to the Roman jail. He saw prisoners packed like cattle in a jail too small to allow them the simplest comfort. And they were so glad to see him! He stayed longer than he should have, and promised to come back.

He had scarcely arrived home before he longed to be with them again. He could see their faces so clearly: the mothers, fathers, little children, and old people; the young lovers who never would walk together again under the soft, spring stars of Rome. He had taught many of them the faith they were about to die for. They needed him. And he went to them. Soon the soldiers noticed that he came to the

prison every day. He was questioned, arrested, and told to sacrifice publicly to the pagan statues in the courtroom. He refused. He was sentenced to death and beheaded on February 14, about the year 270.

Saint Valentine was buried in Rome. One of the gates of the city was at one time named for him: Porto Valentini. A church was built in his honor. And a hiding place for Christians, called a catacomb, was hollowed out of the earth under his grave. But for those who remembered his heroic love and devotion, this was not enough. Gates fall down and churches crumble, in time. Someday there would be no need for catacombs. How could Saint Valentine be remembered forever? What would always remind people to keep his feast day, February 14, after all the early Christians were gone, after all the persecutions were over?

Then someone remembered the birds, the little winged lovers of the sky. Each year on February 14 the birds mate and begin to build their nests in Rome. No edict of an emperor will ever stop them.

And to this day Saint Valentine is remembered by the courtship of the birds. And that is how he became the patron of lovers everywhere, and why his very name has come to mean a love note sent to a loved one on his feast day—a Valentine!

[47]

SAINT ANTONY

THE FIRST ABBOT

"Why don't you stay here, Antony?" his sister asked.

"I don't like cities. There is too much to see. Too much to do. Besides, I am a man. Men can go anywhere."

"And where will you go, Antony?"

"I am going to be a hermit. I'll build a little cell in the woods or in the desert. I've always wanted to."

"I'd be so lonely all by myself."

"But I am lonely here in Memphis."

"Why, Antony?" she asked.

"You might as well know the truth, little sister. There are too many things separating me from God, here. Buildings. People. Noises. Markets. Money."

"Then go where you'll be happiest, dear brother." she said.

In this way Antony and his sister said farewell. The city was Memphis, Egypt. And the time was long ago, in the year 271. Antony was twenty years old.

He and his sister had been born on a farm outside Memphis. They lived there until the death of their parents. Antony then brought his sister to the city. He found a home for her, as happy and as Christian as their farm home had been. He left her enough money to last a lifetime.

When he was sure she was content, he gave all the rest of his father's fortune to the poor. He was penniless when he became a hermit.

In early Christian times hermits were holy men. They felt closer to God when they lived in the wilderness. They slept on straw mats or on the bare earth in caves or cells. For clothing they wore only the skins of animals. They ate only bread and water. They prayed day and night. They were always trying to make up for those who never praised God at all.

For a while Antony's cell was near Memphis. But as word of his holiness grew, more and more people came to him for advice. This left him little time for prayer. When he was thirty-four years old he moved to a ruin on top of a far distant mountain. For twenty years he saw no one, except a man who brought him bread every six months. During that time his breadman brought him many messages. All of them begged him to come down from his mountain and help others. All of them said there was work for him to do among the hermits of Egypt. But Antony knew himself. He felt that he needed this time to make himself truly what he wanted to be: a man as nearly like Jesus as a man could be.

When he was fifty-four years old Antony did come down from his mountain. He gathered all the hermits together and gave them a rule to live by. He took charge of all of them. And he called them monks. This was the most important work of his life. For in this way he founded the first monasteries. He became the first abbot. His example and instructions are a guide rule for monks to this day.

But Antony was always happiest on his lonely mountaintop. There he could pray and do penance without being distracted by others. From there he wrote many beautiful letters to his monks, to emperors, other saints, and ordinary people. These letters were always about God's great love for all of us.

Saint Antony never did any plain visiting. But he went wherever he was needed. And how people loved to have him near them! He seemed to carry happiness in his pockets. He went to Alexandria to comfort the martyrs. He visited the discouraged people in prisons and the sick in hospitals. And somehow he always had the very gift they needed. He gave the martyrs courage. He gave the prisoners hope. He gave the sick strength and friendliness. And in God's name he worked miracles of healing.

Saint Antony lived to be one hundred and five years old. He was strong and vigorous all his life on a diet of bread and water, to which he sometimes added a few dates. Saint Antony died in the solitude he loved, on Mount Kolzim near the Red Sea, on January 15, 356.

SAINT JOHN

THE DWARF

The monastery of Skete was in the very heart of Egypt's wilderness. By day the unshaded sun beat down upon the little church and the cells of the monks that were scattered around it. By night a chilling wind blew across the desert. It was not comfortable country. Yet the monasteries of the desert hermits of Egypt were little islands of peace in the troubled world of the fifth century. There hermits came from many countries. Some were famous and learned men. Others were simple and uneducated. But they all came for the same reason: to feel closer to God, and to worship Him without the interruptions of the world.

In the fourth century Saint Antony had gathered the scattered hermits of Egypt into groups, founded these monasteries, and given the monks a rule to live by. Since then they had drawn men like magnets.

One day the director at Skete was surprised to see a little dwarf at his door. At first he thought he was a little boy, lost in the desert. But John Kolabos soon set him right. He was a young man and he wished to become a monk. As the wise old director looked at him he was not thinking about all the things we wish we knew today about John the Dwarf. He did not ask him who he was or when he was born or where he had come from. (And to this day we do not know. All that we know of John are the stories that have come down to us from the time he entered the monastery at Skete.) The director only wanted to know why John Kolabos wanted to be a monk. John said he wished to follow the example of Christ. The director thought that was a good reason, and admitted him. He noticed that the little dwarf had a quick temper and thought well of himself. But these were human faults and could be overcome.

It is told that his director, wishing to test him, told him to plant a walking stick, and to water it every day until leaves and fruit appeared upon it. Water was faraway, but John carried it each day for three years

[51]

to moisten the earth around his stick. At the end of the third year the rooted stick bore leaves and fruit. His director carried the fruit into church and offered it to the monks; saying: "Take and eat the fruits of obedience."

John knew he was hot-tempered and quick to argue. To rid himself of these faults he refused to talk about the news or any worldly affairs. He kept God so constantly in his mind that often he was absent-minded about his work. He wove baskets in his cell, and sometimes he did not know what his hands were doing. He would weave the reeds for two baskets into one. He would forget things that he was sent for. He was laughed at and scolded. His thoughts on the perfection of God made his own faults shine like headlights in his mind. One by one he put out those lights. His weapons were prayer and fasting, day and night without end. He lost his desire for argument. His temper ceased to flare. He had learned to control himself as well as a fine jockey learns to control the faults of a race horse. Now he began to speak in sermons that held the attention of all. He was able with his words to remove the distance we sometimes feel toward God, and to bring Him close.

It became easy now for him to understand others and help them in their struggles with themselves. We know something of the way he talked to sinners: "What reason can you have to complain of Jesus, that you should thus abandon Him?" he would ask gently. And sinners could not bear the picture his words made. They saw themselves turning from this waiting Friend and quickly ran back to Him.

Strict with himself, John was boundless in his love for others. He loved all sinners as his brothers on earth. He made many converts among them, and among the pagans. Finally he was put in charge of the young men who came to Skete to be monks. Many of them became saints themselves, in following his example.

When the wild Berber tribes of North Africa raided Skete, he was an old man. He escaped by crossing the River Nile toward the Red Sea. He was going on a pilgrimage to Mount Kolzim, where two hundred years before Saint Antony had his hermit cell. Before John died he was asked to leave some words of wisdom for the world. Humbly he denied having wisdom, and said: "I never followed my own will; nor did I ever teach another what I had not first practiced myself."

[53]

SAINT HELENA

PATRON OF THE CROSS

Saint Helena was the mother of Constantine the Great, who ruled the Roman Empire from 307–337.

In those days even state records were not too well kept. People relied on their memories more than they do now. These memories became stories told in homes and on the streets. The history of many heroes and heroines have come down to us this way. Such stories are called legends. And it is through legends that we know Saint Helena.

Usually Roman generals married women of wealth and nobility. But Constantius Chlorus did not. While in Britain with his army he met and married Helena, daughter of a village innkeeper. She went with him on all his early campaigns. At Naissus in Serbia, their son, Constantine was born. As he became ever more powerful in Roman affairs, Constantius was advised to divorce Helena and marry Theodora, a noblewoman. In pagan Rome this was not unusual. Constantius married her and was crowned Emperor of Rome.

Young Constantine always loved and honored Helena, his true mother. When his father died and he became Emperor of the Romans in 307, he proclaimed her Empress. Then in the year 313 he issued the famous Edict of Milan. This law not only allowed but encouraged Christians to preach and practice their faith in peace.

Helena soon became a Christian. She was then about sixty-three years old. Thousands of Romans followed her into the faith. Having once been poor and often neglected, she now used her riches and influence to comfort the old, the sick, and those in need. She built many churches to hold the new Christians. Troubled Romans came to her freely for advice. The people loved her.

Only one thing about the Christians disturbed Helena: they did not have the Cross on which Christ had died. No one even knew where it was. She set out to find it.

In 324 there were two divisions of the Roman Empire, the western, with its capital at Rome, the eastern, with its capital at Byzantium. Each had an emperor. Now Constantine, the Emperor of Rome, became the ruler of both divisions. He moved the capital from Rome to Byzantium, which was called Constantinople in his honor. (This city is now known as Istanbul, Turkey.) Helena was now Empress of the country that held the Holy Land! She became as beloved here as she had been in Rome.

A temple to the pagan goddess Venus had been built outside Jerusalem over the land where Christ had suffered and died. Constantine ordered its removal. Helena then hired diggers to search this sacred earth for the Cross on which Jesus had been crucified. And on May 3, 326 three crosses were found in a dry cistern. But which, if any of them, was Christ's, she wondered?

She consulted Saint Macarius, who was then Bishop of Jerusalem. He suggested they take wood from each of the three crosses into the home of a woman who was near death. He touched the woman with pieces of one cross and then another. Nothing happened. But when he touched her with a part of the third Cross she sat up, bright-eyed and smiling, with her strength fully restored. The wood of the last Cross had told them by a miracle of healing that it was the one that had once held the body of Christ.

Constantine now asked the Bishop of Jerusalem to build a church "worthy of the most marvelous place in the world" on the site where the Cross was found. Although Saint Helena was very old, she joyfully supervised this work to its finish.

While in Palestine she built two more churches: the *Eleona*, on the Mount of Olives, and one where Christ was born, in Bethlehem.

Here too, she performed endless acts of charity. Many were freed from slavery, exile, and suffering by her. Through her the relics of the True Cross were distributed throughout the Christian world. She died in Palestine on August 18, 330.

In honor of the Empress Helena, his mother, Constantine the Great had coins minted with her name on them in Latin: *Flavia Julia Helena.* And because of her, he, too, became a Christian.

[56]

SAINT PATRICIA

THE LITTLE PRINCESS

Most of us think of Patricia as an Irish saint. Many little girls in Ireland, England, the United States, and Canada are named for her. But she was born far away from all these countries, in the land that is now Turkey. She was the daughter of the imperial family of Constantinople, and she lived in the very early days of Christianity.

From the little we know of her life, we can form only a small picture of this sweet young saint. We know she was beautiful, tiny, and graceful. And that she had large dark eyes and long, fine dusky hair. She was carefully educated, richly dressed, and well guarded. And it is thought that at least one of her parents, or her tutor, was Christian, for little Patricia loved and practiced Christian ways from childhood. But when she told her family that she wished to live all of her life for Jesus, they laughed at her. They told her she would think quite differently when she grew up.

In those days a young princess had nothing to say about the man she married. The court made all the arrangements. They selected a worthy young man, usually, and one who would bring the country land and wealth. But when a princess was as lovely as Patricia they could choose among the fairest and the best. And many a fine prince was anxious to marry Patricia. Because her family loved her, they were a long time choosing a husband for her. They wanted her to be happy.

Finally they made their choice. Her husband would be a handsome young nobleman who loved her. He was suitable in all ways. He was rich and kind. Imagine how they felt when Patricia refused to marry him. They could not believe their ears! And when she told them she did not intend to marry anyone on earth at all, they were angry and amazed. But still they did not believe her. They thought that perhaps she was shy. And they went ahead with all the preparations for a great court wedding.

[57]

But one day when they went to find Patricia she was gone. It was a long time before they found out where she was. And then it was too late for the wedding. The prince they had chosen was angry, and he married another wife. The fine jewels and wedding clothes were put away.

Patricia had gone to Italy. In Rome she took vows, consecrating her whole life to God alone. After she had done this, she put on simple clothes and like a little beggar girl she returned to Constantinople. There she gave all her riches to the poor. Her family now realized that she would never take part in the life at court. They offered her a place in the palace where she could live quietly, as she wished. But Patricia felt she had lived in the palace long enough. She felt she should now wait on others and help them. She had seen so many thousands who needed help and love and hope.

Without any money at all she went to Naples, in Italy. And there she worked happily among the very poor, the sick, and the old. She became one of them, sharing their humble, miserable lives. And she did this so quietly that no one knew she had once been a royal princess. Because her body was much frailer than her mind and heart, she did not live long in this poverty. And when she died and was buried, it was as quietly as she had lived. Few paid any attention when the poor of Naples told of miracles that she had wrought among them. But the poor kept their devotion to her. They passed it along from mother to child, from father to son, for centuries.

The relics of Saint Patricia were discovered in 1549. The poor had always visited her burial place, bringing to it the lilies of springtime and the roses of summer. And it was the poor who led to the discovery of her little tomb and the increased devotion to her which spread throughout the world.

Her name is now one of the most popular in the modern world, and it means to be a noble or an aristocrat.

[59]

SAINT CHRISTOPHER

PATRON OF TRAVELERS

Saint Christopher is a very popular saint. You see his image on ships, busses, and trains, on the dashboards of taxicabs and family cars, on the instrument panels of airplanes and submarines, on charm bracelets and key chains, necklaces, and luggage. Often Saint Christopher medals are tucked into purses and wallets or carried in pockets around the world and back again. For Saint Christopher is the patron of travelers. This little legend will tell you why millions who journey by land, air, and water, carry his image with them.

Long, long ago the land that is now Israel, Jordan, Lebanon, and Syria was called the land of Canaan. In the forests of Canaan there lived a giant by the name of Reprobus. He was nineteen-and-a-half feet tall! He was also the strongest man in the world. One day he decided that he would serve only the greatest king in the world. At first he thought the King of Canaan was his man. But the king became frightened one day and Reprobus saw him make the Sign of the Cross.

"Why did you do that?" the giant asked.

"To send the Devil away," the king answered.

"Then you are afraid of the Devil?"

"I am," the king answered.

"Then fare thee well. The Devil is greater than you. I will serve him."

The giant then began to search for the Devil, and he soon found him. He was dressed as a knight. Reprobus served him until, on a walk in the woods one day, he heard the Devil say:

"We must take another road. Let us go back."

"Why?" said the giant.

"There is a wayside Cross on this road."

The giant examined the little shrine. In it he saw only the figure of a poor, naked Man nailed to a Cross.

"This bit of wood carving cannot harm you," said the giant. But the Devil had vanished at the very sight of it.

"If the Devil is afraid of this poor Man with the crown of thorns, then I must find Him and serve Him," the giant said to himself.

He began to look for Jesus. But he did not know His name. In his search he came one evening to a deep river. He waded across it easily. There on the river bank he saw a hermit praying before a wooden Cross. The giant pointed to the crucified Figure:

"There is the Man I seek," he said. "How can I serve Him?"

"Stay here," answered the hermit, "and carry people across the river. He has made you big and strong to help others. In the meantime I will teach you His gentle way."

The giant carried men, women, children, heavily laden horses and camels across the river on his mighty shoulders. Nothing tired him. To this nineteen-and-a-half foot giant all things were light as feathers.

One night he wakened from sleep to hear a small voice calling him: "Ferryman! Ferryman! Will you carry me over?"

He came out of his hut and saw a little Child waiting at the shore.

"Am I too heavy for you, ferryman?"

Reprobus laughed and tossed the Child to his back. Then taking his staff he stepped into the black water. When he had gone a little way the Child began to grow heavier and heavier. The giant's shoulders began to droop and ache. His arms swelled and strained. His straight back bent, and he thought his legs would buckle.

"Child," he said. "I never carried so great a burden. I feel as though I had the world on my shoulders."

Finally he stumbled to the bank. Gently he put the Child down on dry land. Then he fell wearily onto the grass.

The Child looked at him lovingly. His hands touched the giant's ragged head. Then He said: "Reprobus, you have just carried the world and the One who created the world upon thy shoulders."

When the giant looked up, the Child had vanished. Filled with happiness, he knew that he had met the greatest King at last. He placed

his lips on the ground where the Child had stood, and whispered: "My Master!"

And when he had learned all the teachings of Jesus from the hermit, he was baptized and called Christopher, which means Christ-bearer.

SAINT ALBAN

THE MASQUERADER AND FIRST MARTYR OF ENGLAND

Hundreds of years ago England was ruled by the Romans and it was called Britannia. The policemen were Roman soldiers. Most of the people were pagans.

In the year 284, Diocletian became Emperor of the Romans. He ordered his soldiers to search his entire empire for Christians, and to kill all they found.

At this time there was a town in southeast Britannia called Verulamium. It was in what is now the county of Hertfordshire, near London. One of its most important citizens was a man named Alban.

One stormy night he heard a knock on his door. When he answered it, a priest gasped out of the darkness: "The Roman soldiers are looking for me! Will you hide me for a few days? I will give you no trouble."

Alban was kind. But there was a law forbidding anyone to help Christians. However, he had never heard of any harm they had done. And this fellow looked so tired and cold.

"Come in," he said, and bolted the door against the storm.

He began to like the priest. He asked about his work. The priest told him he was trying to bring the love of Christ into all hearts. He told Alban about Jesus' great love of man. Alban began to compare Christ to his pagan gods. Christ was kind, and they were cruel. Christ was a gift-giver, and they were greedy. In the few days they had together, Alban learned about the religion of Jesus, and became a Christian.

House by house the Roman soldiers were searching the city, looking for the priest. Late one night Alban heard their heavy boots at his door. The priest stood up: "They've come for me," he said, "and my work is not yet finished. Britannia needs Christ."

Then he put on his cloak, and turning to Alban, he said: "Thank you for helping me. Hold to your faith. God will be with you. I am not afraid to die."

[63]

"Wait!" whispered Alban, snatching the priest's cloak from him. "Take my jacket and escape. I'll pretend to be you."

In the priest's cloak Alban answered the door. The soldiers took him away. When the governor saw who he was he became very angry. He knew Alban had many friends. He ordered him to sacrifice to the pagan gods. Alban refused. He said they were false gods and he no longer believed in them. The governor ordered him to be scourged. Alban smiled during the terrible lashing. This made the governor angrier than before. He asked Alban if he were a Christian. Alban said that he was. Now the governor sentenced him to be beheaded. He thought this would teach the people not to play jokes upon their Roman rulers. But Alban's friends did not desert him.

Most of the townfolk followed him to the place where he was to die. Walking alongside him was the soldier who was to cut off his head. Halfway there he threw his sword to the ground and asked to die instead of Alban or to die with him.

The big procession climbed Holmhurst Hill, outside the town. It was summertime. The grass was filled with wild flowers. Alban was weak and thirsty. He asked God for a drink of water. As he prayed a clear, cold spring burst from the earth at his feet. Refreshed, Alban walked bravely to his death. A few minutes later the soldier who had refused to kill him was also beheaded.

In honor of this brave, kind man the people changed the name of their city to Saint Albans. And Holmhurst Hill became Holywell Hill. And pagan Britannia began to become Christian England.

SAINT AGNES

THE GIRL MARTYR

In the year 303, Diocletian, Emperor of Rome published his edict against Christians. This meant that they were to be arrested and brought to trial. When they were captured he made fun of them and ordered them to promise to give up the worship of their God. All who refused he sentenced to death. And most of them refused.

With soldiers looking everywhere for Christians, there was much excitement in Rome. People talked about how much these Christians loved one another. And about how bravely they died. Many pagans said they had seen them smiling happily as they were thrown to hungry lions in the amphitheater in Rome.

There was a nobleman in Rome at this time who had a little daughter named Agnes. She was considered to be the most beautiful and charming of all the noble Roman girls. Her riches and her personal loveliness excited the admiration of all the young Roman nobles. Each of them hoped to marry her someday.

Agnes was just twelve years old when she began to wonder about Christianity. What sort of a god could make people so happy in their love, that they would rather die than give Him up, she asked herself. And when she found out, she too, fell completely in love with Jesus and His gentle teachings. Secretly, she promised her life to Him.

One of the young nobles who was in love with her became very angry when she told him she would never marry. He was so furious at her refusal of him, that he told the Emperor Diocletian that she had become a Christian. Immediately the emperor sent for Agnes. Gently he asked her to prove to him the foolishness of what he had been told, by worshiping the pagan gods. This she refused to do. Even cruel Diocletian could not at first sentence this beauty to death. She was so young and the blood of powerful Romans ran through her veins. When all his pleadings failed, he tried to frighten her. He had the instruments

of torture shown to her. She held fast to her faith. Then he had her punished severely, hoping she would change her mind. But Agnes did not change her mind. Enraged at his failure, Diocletian ordered her to be killed.

But even this did not frighten her. She died like the little noble Roman that she was, for the God she believed in. All this happened in the year 304, when both Christianity and Agnes were very young. She was just thirteen years old at the time of her martyrdom.

In the year 354 a church on the Via Nomentana in Rome was built in her honor. Each year in her church on her feast day, while the choir is singing her praises, two white lambs are placed in the sanctuary. They are blessed and cared for until it is time to shear them. Out of their wool are woven soft shoulder scarves, called pallia. These are sent as gifts to the archbishops in remembrance of Saint Agnes.

SAINT AMBROSE

LAWYER AND BISHOP

In the year 340 the land we know as France was called Gaul. It was part of the Roman Empire and ruled by a pagan scholar, the Prefect Ambrose. In this year his last child, a son, was born at Trier. He, too, was called Ambrose.

Young Ambrose never really knew his famous father, for the Prefect died while he was still a baby. His mother returned to Rome with her children. Ambrose grew up among the nobles and scholars of the city. He learned Greek and Latin. He became a poet, orator, grammarian, and lawyer. When he was only thirty-four years old he was chosen by the emperor to fill one of the most important posts of empire. He was made governor of two powerful provinces, with his residence in Milan, Italy.

Ambrose was studying to be a Christian when he moved to Milan. But he was not yet baptized. On his arrival he found the city troubled over the election of a new bishop. To secure peace under his rule and to introduce himself to the people, Ambrose entered the city just before the election was to take place. He planned to advise those present to keep their tempers and to select their bishop wisely. His moving words and his noble bearing pleased the people so much that before he had finished his speech one of them cried: "Ambrose, bishop!"

Everyone took up this cry and the new Roman governor was elected the new Bishop of Milan! Ambrose was thunderstruck. He tried to escape. He wrote to the emperor asking him to issue an order excusing him. But the emperor was proud that his appointed governor had been so honored. He refused to issue the order. Ambrose was baptized a Christian and consecrated Bishop of Milan. Immediately he broke all ties with his old world. He gave his fortune to the church, his jewels, clothing, and furniture to the poor. He began to study Holy Scripture and Church Law, and was ordained a priest. To this office he brought

[69]

his whole being, all of his brilliant mind and loving heart. His churches were always filled, crowds overflowing into the streets when he preached. He became far more powerful as a bishop that he would ever have been as governor. His well-trained legal mind enabled him to protect his people and their church property from all threats with authority and justice.

Augustine, a famous teacher, was in Milan at this time. He was coming, after much struggle, to the end of his search for truth. This man, who was to become a saint and one of the greatest champions Christianity has ever known, was greatly impressed by Ambrose. They were both scholars. In his sermons to the people of Milan, Ambrose was giving what one day Augustine would give to the world in books: a Christian knowledge of the worth and purpose of man. Saint Augustine and his little son were baptized by Ambrose.

Fortunately, many examples of the Bishop of Milan's justice and love of men have come down to us: At one time he was criticized for having the golden vessels of the church melted down to ransom captives of the Goths. His reply was quick and pointed: "If the church possesses gold it is in order to use it for the needy, not to keep it."

Even the Emperor Theodosius, whom Ambrose loved, felt his wrath. When he attempted to interfere in church affairs, the Bishop of Milan reminded him that he was a civil and not a religious ruler with these words: "The emperor is *in* the church, not *over* it!"

When Theodosius ordered the massacre of seven thousand people at Thessalonica, Ambrose ordered him to do a public penance for this horrible act, saying: "What he has done at Thessalonica is unparalleled in the memory of man!"

Emperor Theodosius did the public penance. But these two great men, holding separate authorities, remained friends. Theodosius died in the arms of Ambrose. Two years after the death of the emperor, Ambrose fell ill and foretold the time of his own death. Hearing that he was dying, Count Stilicho, guardian of the Emperor's son said: "The day that this man dies, destruction hangs over Italy." Ambrose died on Good Friday, April 4, 397. He was about fifty-seven years old. He was buried on Easter Sunday and his relics rest under the high altar of his church, the Cathedral of Milan, where they were placed in the year 835.

SAINT MARTIN OF TOURS

THE SOLDIER SAINT

In the fourth century Hungary was called Pannonia. And France was called Gaul. In the town of Sabaria in Pannonia there lived a brave fifteen-year-old lad who wished to become a Christian monk. His name was Martin.

When his father heard of Martin's wish he enrolled his son in the Roman army. The strictness of the life appealed to the boy, but he hated the violence of war. Nevertheless, in three years he was made an officer under Julian, commander of the Roman army.

When Julian led the Romans into Gaul, Martin was with him. He rode a fine horse and wore a handsome scarlet cloak over his armor. He stood his horse at the gates of the city of Amiens to let his foot soldiers pass. The day was cold and a naked beggar cried for comfort in Christ's name at the gate. As Martin rode through his eyes met the beggar's. Martin had nothing to give him. But with his sword he cut his cloak in two and let half of it fall upon the poor beggar. That night he dreamed he saw Christ wearing his half cloak in heaven. When he wakened from this sweet dream he made up his mind to wait no longer to join himself to Jesus. He was baptized a Christian that day.

For two more years he fought in the Roman army. Then came the time when he could not take another life. He felt that God had made men for far better things. He asked to be released before another battle was fought. Julian refused, called him a coward, and threw him into prison. But soon an envoy of the enemy came to Julian's camp and asked for peace. It was granted, and the battle Martin refused to fight was never fought at all. Julian released him. Martin was twenty

years old.

Martin now went to Poitiers and became a disciple of Saint Hilary. He lived for ten years as a hermit and preacher, and during this time he founded the monastery at Ligugé. But it was useless for him to hope for a humble life. He could not hide the radiance of his face or his silver tongue. People clung to him, crowded the churches where he spoke, followed him in the streets. In Tours they demanded him as bishop.

Martin found much to do as Bishop of Tours. He fought falsehood with truth. He uprooted all the old superstitions which blocked the understanding of Christ's teaching.

Great legends grew up around him.

It is said that he met the Devil one day on the road to Rome. The Devil said. "Good morning, monk. Is it the Bishop of Tours?"

"You are not mistaken," Martin answered.

"What a poor Master you must serve who cannot provide a better means of travel."

"He can!" shouted Martin. In that instant he changed the Devil into a mule, jumped on his back, and rode him to Rome. Soon the Devil was panting, but whenever he showed signs of slowing down, Martin made the sign of the Cross over him. And this made the Devil run harder than ever.

Another time it is said he destroyed a pagan temple and was about to chop down the tree outside it. The pagans said they would do the chopping for him if Martin would consent to stand where the tree would fall. For, they argued, if his God were the true one, He would not let him be injured. Martin agreed. The pagans bound him to the spot. The tree began to topple in his direction. Martin made the sign of the Cross, and just as it was about to crush him, the great tree fell clear of him.

Now Martin made a hiding place for himself at Marmoutier on the banks of the River Loire. His forest cell was shut in by high cliffs and woods. Eighty monks became his disciples there. Each had a cave. Each wore a garment of animal skins, took no wine, and ate just once a day. Whenever Martin was free of his duties as bishop, he came to Marmoutier. The monks sat at his feet to learn from him. And it is said that a young escaped slave, who was later to be as great a saint as Martin, was one of those monks. His name was Patrick.

Martin had such reverence for God's gift of life that he protected pagans and heretics from persecution. He opposed Church authority for using civil power and the death penalty against them.

[73]

In 397, at an age of more than eighty years Saint Martin died in Candes, where the Loire and Vienne rivers join. According to an old legend, his body was placed on a boat without oars or sails and it floated *upstream* to Tours. It is said that on this journey the trees on the river banks burst into flower, and there was heavenly music in the air.

France holds no relic dearer than Martin's scarlet half cloak. Her kings rode into battle with it fluttering before them. In France to this day his feast, called Martinmas, is kept on November 11. And throughout the land the first of the wine harvest is drunk in honor of St. Martin of Tours.

SAINT AUGUSTINE

THE TEACHER

"A whipping is what he needs. The lad's too fresh," said one of the old men sitting on a bench in the market square of Tagaste in North Africa. But even as he said it he smiled, thinking of the splendid young strength of the boy.

"He'll never get it. That one can talk himself out of all blame. His father thinks he will rule Carthage someday. And many agree with him," his companion answered.

It was the year 370 and North Africa was ruled by the Romans. The two old men were talking about Augustine, son of Patricius, a Roman official of the town. Most of Tagaste was talking about him these days. Teachers from Madaura, the finest school for miles around, said that the boy had an amazing brain. He had learned all they could teach him in one year, and impishly asked for more. He was ready for the university while other boys his age were still doing simple sums. Now he was home again, and restless. All the lads in town were at his heels, for Augustine was a gay and exciting companion. His brain bubbled with ideas, and these ideas often turned into mischief.

Augustine's home life was strange. His father was a pagan, an ambitious and rather dull man. His mother, Monica, was a gentlewoman and a Christian. But she was too sad for his taste. When she wasn't scolding him, she was praying for him. Augustine defied her whenever she asked him to moderate his life. He fought off all her efforts to bring him into her faith. He was eager to be away from both of them, off on his own at the university in Carthage.

At Carthage he soon became the idol of the university, its finest speaker and writer. And there he became converted to a faith his mother loathed. Never given to half measures, he began to teach and preach this faith.

In these years he began to turn away from foolish companions and seek the company of scholars. He became dissatisfied with his new faith. He gave it up. He searched and found flaws in all the religions he examined. He felt empty. But there was one belief he avoided. This was Christianity, the faith of his mother.

When Augustine finished his studies at Carthage he made his living as a teacher, and he became a famous one. It was while he was teaching in Milan, Italy, that he met Ambrose, Bishop of Milan. He admired *this* man. It was here, and in association with Ambrose, that Augustine saw a wonderful public act of faith. Roman soldiers had come to seize the cathedral. But they could not even approach it without killing thousands of Christians who had decided to protect it, and the bishop inside it, by making a human carpet of themselves. Their prostrate bodies surrounded the cathedral square and spread out for blocks along the street. The second time he saw this happen there were more Roman soldiers and more people guarding their church and its pastor in the same manner. The Roman soldiers withdrew both times before this vast human protest. Augustine visited Ambrose to learn the source of this devotion. But Ambrose was too busy teaching the ignorant and caring for the needy to spend much time with a scholar able to find his own way through the mazes of the mind. He advised him to read the Scriptures. Not for beautiful writing, but for beautiful ideas.

In the Scriptures, Augustine found no flaws. But there was one thing he could never understand: Christ's unending love for us. Why did He bother, Augustine wondered?

Augustine had been loved by many in his life. But he had never really loved anyone. For, in love, one gives up one's own desire to please another. Augustine never admired anyone enough to do that, until he found Christ.

On Easter Sunday in 386, Augustine was baptized and confirmed by Saint Ambrose, Bishop of Milan. He was thirty-two years old, and Monica, his mother, was present. A little poem that he wrote tells how he felt on that day:

> *Late have I loved thee,*
> *O Beauty so ancient and so new;*
> *Late have I loved thee.*

From that time on Augustine belongs to history. He was the first *great* Christian philosopher. He founded the Augustinian order. He became a priest and the Bishop of Hippo, in Africa. He worked miracles. He wrote books that are classics, his *Confessions* and *The City of God*. Saint Augustine died on August 28 in the year 430, in the city of Hippo in Africa.

His last words come down to us, important in any age but particularly in our own: "My greatest folly . . . I wanted . . . to understand *everything*."

He had discovered that beyond understanding there is the mystery of God's love for us and the grace and faith that flow from it.

SAINT DOROTHEA
THE GIVER OF APPLES AND ROSES

Everything in this story happened in Cappadocia in the fourth century. Cappadocia was an important city in Asia Minor, in what is now Turkey.

Theophilus, the young Mayor, admired Sapricius, the Governor, very much. When Sapricius had criminals in court, Theophilus often watched him conduct the trials. One day as he entered the courtroom, Sapricius said to him:

"Today I am trying Christians. They always say the same thing. They are always willing to die. These trials are a bore."

"I'm free until the banquet tonight. I'll stay awhile and amuse myself."

One after another Theophilus saw the tired Christians come before the Governor. One after another they were sentenced to death.

"Next!" the Governor kept calling, impatiently.

Suddenly Theophilus leaned forward in his chair as a prisoner entered. She was young and fresh and beautiful. She walked as proudly as a princess. Flowers and ribbons were woven into her golden hair.

"Your name," snapped the Governor.

"Dorothea of Caesarea."

It would be wrong for a girl so beautiful to die, thought Theophilus. The Christians were fools to throw their lives away so lightly. He leaned forward, listening.

"Don't you fear death at all?" the Governor asked.

"Why should I fear it? It will bring me to the One I love."

"And who is that?"

"His name is Jesus."

[80] Theophilus could not bear to see her die. The others, perhaps: the old and poor and weary. But not this lovely one! He spoke to her: "How can you bear to leave the flowers and the sunshine. All of earth's delights?" he said.

She turned and smiled at him. "Tell me your name," she said.

"Theophilus."

"In Heaven, Theophilus, it is always the sweetest part of summertime. The lilies bloom and the roses never fade. On the tall, eternal trees the apples are ruby and gold among the shining leaves. And the river waters sing."

"Since Heaven is such a fine place, you shall go there today," shouted the Governor.

As Dorothea passed the place where Theophilus was sitting, he leaned toward her and said, mockingly, "Send me some apples and roses from Paradise."

"I will," she answered, smiling.

"And what have you done with yourself, today?" friends asked Theophilus at the banquet that night.

"I listened to Sapricius sentencing Christians. And a miracle was promised me."

Everyone laughed.

"Yes, a maid said she would send me apples and roses from Paradise. She was about to die."

"Those crazy Christians!" someone shouted. And they all laughed. But suddenly the laughter ended, for into the banquet hall came an angelic little child, carrying three apples and three roses. They were of such fragrance and perfection as was never seen before in Cappadocia. The child gave them to Theophilus, and said: "Dorothea sends you these." Theophilus took them. The child vanished.

The next day Sapricius was trying Christians.

"Next?" he said, and "Name?"

"Theophilus of Cappadocia."

"What foolishness is this?" the Governor cried.

"No jest, Sapricius."

"Why are you here?"

"Because I believe in Dorothea's God."

"Think, Theophilus. You may be governor some day. Give up this madness."

"I have given up all madness."

"Then you belong in Paradise with Dorothea. Go now, fool."

And the soldiers led Theophilus to the execution place.

SAINT DOROTHEA

SAINT APOLLO

THE JOYOUS ONE

Southeast of Greece, in the Aegean Sea, there are more than two hundred Greek islands. If you look at them from an airplane, you see them as a flower-shape in the water. The smallest island is the heart of them, and the large ones form a circle, like petal tips around it. These islands are called the Cyclades. The capital city of this land-and-water world is Hermopolis, on the island of Siros.

These islands and this city were famous long before Christ was born. Hermopolis is still an important seaport. Olives and grapes grown in its dry, rich soil are prized for their size and flavor all over the world. But Hermopolis is famous for more than its choice olives and grapes. Saint Apollo spent the last years of his life there.

Apollo was almost eighty years old when he came to Hermopolis. But he did not look it. He was strong and quick, with a spring in his step and a smile on his face. He had spent many years as a hermit before coming to Hermopolis.

When he saw the holy men in the city going around with sad and worried faces, he gathered them all together. He formed a community of monks, and he gave them a rule to live by. It must have been a very good rule, for hundreds of young men joined the order while he lived. And the people of the city flocked to hear him when he preached. He made goodness an exciting, happy thing.

"It is not alway easy to be good," he would say to them. "But when you make a prayer of it, and send each act of goodness to God as a little gift, then it is not so difficult. And whenever God sees your little gift, He will not be outdone. He will send you a finer one. Just try it, and very soon your hearts will be filled with happiness."

One part of his rule he repeated each day to his monks. And they in turn told the people of Hermopolis. This is the rule: "A sad and

melancholy look does not become a Christian. Of all people, Christians should have cheerful hearts. And they should have cheerful faces, too. How can you frown when you know God loves you? He has no need for grapes and olives. They are all for you. He does not need the sun or the sea or the hills. They are all for you. There is only one time when you should be sad. That is when you are ashamed because you have broken one of God's laws. But if you are really sorry you have hurt Him, He is quick to understand and forgive."

Apollo knew how to give people hope. "Now, how would you feel,"

he would say, "if you gave many gifts to someone and they went around looking grumpy? You would think they didn't love you, wouldn't you? You would feel they didn't care for your gifts, wouldn't you? Then lift up your faces and smile. Not only the earth is for you. God has heaven waiting for you, too. Smile for happiness, you Christians."

This holy man robed all his monks in white. And, though the cloth was coarse, the robes were as bright as purity. And it was pleasant to see the smiling monks in their light robes flashing through the city streets.

Many are the tales told of Saint Apollo. Miracle upon miracle is credited to him. But there is one more popular than all the others. There was a famine in Hermopolis. The people were near starvation. Saint Apollo did not have many loaves in his monastery. But he took what he had and blessed them. He told his monks to pass them out as far as they would go, to ease the hunger of the people. The famine lasted for four months, and so did the bread. The baskets were never empty. The bread was always fresh.

"There is no end to God's goodness." Saint Apollo said, smiling, when the people came to thank him. "He sent you bread because he loves you. I merely asked Him for it."

Saint Apollo was more than ninety years old when he died, in the year 395.

SAINT NICHOLAS

PATRON OF GREECE

Today, the peninsula of western Asia is called Turkey. When Saint Nicholas lived it was called Asia Minor. This country was one of the oldest, richest, and most civilized in the world. It was divided into many kingdoms. One of them was called Lycia.

Saint Nicholas was born in the city of Patara in Lycia, in the fourth century. His parents were wealthy nobles, and they were Christians.

It is a wonder that Nicholas became a saint. He was one of the most loved and indulged children who ever lived. His home was beautiful. His parents and servants gave him far more of everything than he needed. He had every toy there was. He had the best of clothing and of food. The finest scholars were hired to teach him. He had his own clowns to entertain him, and enough performing animals to make a circus. His parents died when he was a very young man, and they left him a great fortune.

Usually, when one has so much, one becomes selfish, or is lost in the enjoyment of what one has and does not see the need of others. But not Saint Nicholas. All his life he shared all of the blessings God showered down upon him. He felt that God trusted him to find and help the needy ones. And to Saint Nicholas the needy ones were not only those who did not have enough to eat or to wear. They were also the ones whose minds and hearts were poor and empty. These he filled with a love and knowledge of Jesus. Saint Nicholas did all these things in such a pleasing way that people never forgot him. For more than sixteen hundred years the legends of Saint Nicholas have kept his memory bright. Here is one of them:

When Saint Nicholas was a young priest he wanted to see the place where Christ was crucified. He decided to cross the Mediterranean Sea to Alexandria, Egypt, and to go from there overland to Jerusalem. When his ship was halfway across the water a terrible storm arose.

The sky darkened. Lightning flashed like swords in the sky. Great waves smashed against the ship. It began to break up. In one of the lightning flashes, the captain saw Nicholas kneeling in prayer.

"We are all past praying for now, priest. Get up and I'll lash you to the mast. That way you may be saved," he said.

"Nothing is ever past praying for," Saint Nicholas said calmly.

As he said these words the sun came out. The wind stopped howling. The angry sea became smooth and flat.

"Who are you, priest?" the captain said.

"I am Nicholas," he answered.

Then the captain turned to his astonished crew and said: "Remember that name, men. If ever we are near death on the sea, call on Nicholas. He will save us."

And the sailors remembered. And they told others. And others told others, until this day.

All over Europe in the seaport churches you will see finely hand-carved, little sailing ships tacked to the walls or hanging from the rafters. They are all well rigged and trimmed. These have been made lovingly for centuries by sailors. After long voyages and safe landfalls they have been left as thank-you offerings to Saint Nicholas, the patron of all who sail the sea in ships.

Another legend tells us of a poor nobleman with three beautiful daughters. Each was loved by a fine young man. But their father could not provide dowries for them. Without a dowry in those days no girl could hope for marriage. Three times in the darkness of night Nicholas threw purses filled with gold into the nobleman's study. And not until the last time did the poor nobleman discover who had turned sorrow into happiness in his home.

Nicholas swore him to secrecy. But such joyous secrets are rarely kept. Perhaps the girls teased, or the nobleman gave hints too broad to be mistaken. But one told another in all languages and so today this tale is in the folklore of the world.

Saint Nicholas is patron of Greece, co-patron with Saint Andrew of Russia. Sicily in Italy, Lorraine in France, and Galway in Ireland claim him, too.

[88]

SAINT PATRICK

PATRON OF IRELAND

The boy with his hands bound behind his back was chained to other slaves on the deck of the pirate ship. He had been in the dark hold so long that now the daylight blinded him. Blinking, he saw land ahead.

"This is where I will be sold as a slave," he thought.

Beyond the shoreline the earth wore the greenest-green he had ever seen. Above it, in the distance, rose the hills and mists and the mountains of the Antrim coast of Ireland.

Along with other slaves he was jerked ashore. As soon as his feet touched land, a powerful chieftain grabbed him. He slapped and pawed and punched every inch of the boy's body to see if he was strong and sound.

"How much for this one, anyhow?" he said, sneering at the boy as if he were worthless.

"The best comes high," the slave trader snapped. "This one's strong as a bull. Pay, or leave go of him and let the others have a look."

Bargaining for this one was useless. For he was far and away the best of the lot for sale. A fine, big broth of a boy he was, with promise of a prime man already on him. Growling, the chieftain tossed the price of him to the ship's captain.

"What are ye called, lad?" he said, shoving him into a cart.

"Patricius Magonus Sucatus," the boy answered.

"Fetched from . . . ?"

"Bannavem Taberniae. I was hunting in my father's wood. The pirates came on me from behind."

"A Roman, be ye?"

"My father is Calpurnius, a deacon and Roman official. My mother is Conchessa, and French."

"Be ye Christian?"

"I am."

[89]

"Away with it all. Ye be Patrick, the slave, now, the pig tender."

It was the fifth century. Ireland was a wild, pagan country. Many of the Picts in the north were pirates and slave traders. They saw nothing wrong in this work. They were big, brave men who wore bright tattoos on their skin. Their pagan religion had no love in it. No thought for another's misfortune. It was cruel, and held the people by fear.

For seven years Patrick tended pigs on Slemish Mountain. He was often cold and hungry. It was then that he came to love Jesus so much. For Jesus was all he had left from home. And compared to the gods the Irish worshiped, Jesus was a marvel of love. He talked to Him through all his loneliness. He spoke to Him in the old prayers he knew. And he made up new ones for comfort. Now all he wanted was to be free, so that he could become a priest.

His master showed him no kindness. But his master was only one man. He met hundreds of others. And they charmed him. They were like the wild fern in their ways: tough and touchy, sensitive and sweet. Their tempers were hot and quick. Their love was deep and strong. And they had dreams of a fine, graceful world. Soon he learned to speak their tongue as well as if he had been born among them. And he slipped into their ways of doing and thinking. Patrick became an Irishman!

There were only two things in this country that he hated. And he always thought of them together: the deadly snakes that slithered

through the moist green fields, and the evil power of the pagan priests over the people.

One night he had a dream. In it he heard a voice saying: "Run away, Patrick. A ship is waiting to take you home!"

The next night Patrick escaped. He ran through the darkness to the Irish coast. There, as the dream promised, a ship was about to sail for France. He had no money, but he promised the captain his parents would pay his passage and he was taken aboard.

After a perilous journey they arrived at Patrick's old home. There was much rejoicing. The sailors were paid and fed and they departed. Patrick's family told him of their great plans for him. But he was restless. He wanted to become a priest. He missed the land of his slavery. He was twenty-three years old. Tenderly he said farewell to his family. He went to France. There, we are told, he lived in a cave like a hermit, and studied under the great monk-teacher, Martin of Tours. He became a priest, then a bishop. All the while he longed for Ireland.

And then one happy day Patrick was chosen to head a mission back to the land of his slavery!

It is not easy to change the faith of a nation. And it was not easy for Saint Patrick. But gradually the wonder of him worked through the land. Everywhere there was talk of him.

"The love of him," the people said. "To leave his own and become one of us."

"The marvel of him," they said. "He challenged the pagan priests to a trial of magic, and he won."

"The greatness of him," the people said. "He drummed the snakes out of Ireland into the sea."

"The pure wisdom of him," they cried. "With the little shamrock he explains the Trinity."

"The power of him," they boasted. "He brings us heaven and ends the sting of death."

Under Saint Patrick the whole country became Christian.

Saint Patrick was a very old man when he died. Some say he was seventy-six. Others swear he lived to be one hundred and twenty. Some say he comes back every Easter Eve, and that at midnight, if the wind is right, you can hear him singing hallelujahs in the Irish hills. It is indeed safe to say he will live in Irish hearts forever.

SAINT COLMAN

AND HIS THREE LITTLE HELPERS

Anyone will tell you that the finest fishing nets and sea ropes come from Connacht, Ireland. And everyone knows the best fishermen in Connacht are the Galway County men. For the sea has hugged their land for centuries, and they know its ways better than most.

They tell great tales in Galway. Tales about the sea, and those who take their living from it. Tales about those who fish for cod, and about the Galway saints who fished for souls for God. And it's then you'll hear about Colman, the Galway boy. They tell of him best on nights when the fog rolls in from Galway Bay. For the fog and the mists blot out the present, and it's easy to think the old times are back again.

Colman was born, they'll tell you, in Kiltartan. His hair was gold as the sun. His eyes were blue as the summer sea. And he was cousin to Guaire, King of Connacht. He was like any lad to begin with. They say he was a bit spoiled from all the love around him. His mother held his mug while he drank. His father carried him on his shoulders through the streets. His aunt curled his hair around her finger. His nurse pulled him through the woods in a cart until her old arms ached. Things went on like that until he was a big boy. Then he changed.

It was Jesus caused the change in him. From a great talker he became a quiet boy. He turned from greediness to giving everything he had to the poor. He wanted to please Jesus in all that he did. When he was praying he wanted no one around. Even the sound of the cook's pans bothered him. He took off to the woods then, to pray in the quiet. But the people found him there. He told them he was the world's worst sinner. But they knew better. They wanted him to lead them in holiness. He felt he was not good enough. But he was helpless against their talk. He was made their bishop. They thought he could not leave them, now. But he did. He fled to the mountains in County Clare. There in the green peace he was alone with God for many years. He lived on

[93]

water and wild vegetables. There he fought many battles with Satan, the tempter. There he grew strong. So strong the devil could not tempt him any more.

They say he had three little friends for company: a rooster, a mouse, and a fly.

He fed grain to the rooster. And in return, at daybreak every morning, the rooster came close to his ear and cried: "Cook-a-doodle-do!" That's the way he wakened Colman in time for his morning prayers.

A little velvety mouse visited Colman every night. If he did not waken, the mouse nibbled his ear. Colman rose and thanked him. For he loved to praise God in the night, while others slept.

One day a fly sat on Colman's prayer book. Colman fed it and said: "Little friend, will you mark my place in my prayer book?" From then on whenever Colman had to leave his prayers, the fly kept his place on the page. He did this by sitting on the very last word Colman had read.

Colman might have spent the rest of his life praising God on the mountain. But a strange thing happened.

They say that on Easter Day, King Guaire of Connacht sat down to his dinner. But angels took it from under his nose and carried it away. The king tried to follow them. But they were too quick for him. Then he rode off in the direction they had taken. After a long time he came to the hut where Colman lived. Colman had shared his feast with his forest friends. But the king knew his empty dishes when he saw them. And there they were, in Colman's hut. He knew then that his cousin Colman was a saint. He gave him land in a place called Kilmacduagh. And Saint Colman built a monastery there. He felt ready to help others to holiness, now. With God's help he would act as the first bishop of Kilmacduagh.

He is loved throughout Ireland to this day. And beyond Ireland, too. Wherever in the world there are Galway men, you'll find the name Colman among them.

All this happened they'll tell you in Galway, about fourteen hundred years ago.

SAINT BRIGID

THE GIVE-AWAY SAINT

This is the story of Brigid, or Bride, as she is sometimes called, as it has come down to us from the legends of the golden age in Ireland.

In the middle of the fifth century, farmer Dubtach of Faughart paused in his field to worry about his beautiful daughter, Brigid. He loved her dearly, but what could be done about her? When she was a child it was only small things she gave away to the beggars: a mug of milk or a toy, bits of bread and cabbage or the dress she was wearing. But since she had become a young woman the beggars had worn a path to his door. And if Brigid was at home, and they asked in God's name, they got what they came for: the last bit of food in the house, any clothes not on the family backs, any coin not spent, any jewel not hidden, went into the beggars' hands. Soon she would have the house empty and the farm stripped down to the bare earth.

And she was so beautiful, it broke the heart to look at her! Fair as an angel, she was, with a laughing face, a skin like milk spilled over roses and heaven's own blue for eyes!

The girl must have a husband, he thought, to take the burden of all this giving from her poor father. And a fine husband would not be hard to find with the cream of the lads from all around gaping with joy at the very sight of her! Having made up his mind to find her a husband, farmer Dubtach sent at once for a fine young noble, and bid Brigid pretty herself for him.

"But, 'tis a nun's veil I'm wanting, Da," she said.

"And 'tis a wedding veil you'll be taking," he answered.

[96] Brigid ran to her room. Here, instead of arranging her hair and her dress for a lover, she asked God to take her beauty, if it was to separate her from Him, her only love.

Trusting Him completely, she came down to meet her suitor. Her hair was dry as stacked hay. Her skin was lined as an old woman's. And one of her eyes was gone! In a cracked voice she whispered to the lad, begging him to refuse her as his wife. She had no need to beg, for the young man found her horrible to look upon, and he went away.

Her poor father was beside himself when he saw her. Knowing that no man would ever want her for a wife now, he listened to her pleas to become a nun. In spite of her generosity to the beggars and her present ugliness, he knew he would miss her dreadfully. But he gave his permission, and off she went with three companions. As soon as the bishop had given her the white habit of a nun all of her beauty came back! She was a very vision of womanhood.

She and her companions now journeyed until they found a sweet green plain where a tall oak tree spread out its great wide arms for shade. In the shelter of this tree Brigid built her cell. Now she was the Bride of Christ, and she could welcome the beggars freely in His name, as He would wish her to do.

But more than beggars came to know the beautiful white nun. And they called her home, Kil-dara, the cell of the oak. Many who visited her were eager to live a life like hers. Holy men and holy women came to her, and whole families. Soon a city grew up on the green plain, and it was called Kildare.

It is told that one day after an April shower, Brigid came into her cell and dropped her wet scarf on a sunbeam. Supposing it to be a beam of wood, she thought no more about it. When the sun went down, the little sunbeam stayed on in the cell, still holding the scarf. Not until twilight had turned into night and Brigid, feeling a chill, put on the scarf again did the little sunbeam rush through the dark night to join the sun.

Saint Brigid loved the sun. She thought it was God's greatest gift to earth. It is said that one evening a little blind girl, Dara, sat with her, and as the sun set they spoke of God's sweet love and care of all His creatures. Forgetting time, they were still talking when the sun rose the next day behind the Wicklow mountains, spreading the sky with gold and making diamonds of the dew. Thrilled with the splendor of this morning that Dara could not see, Brigid whispered a prayer and touched the blind girl's eyes. Instantly Dara saw the golden morning. For a little while she looked upon this shining glory. Then she said softly: "Close my eyes again, mother. While my eyes behold the world, I cannot see God with my soul."

Brigid said another little prayer, and sight passed from Dara's eyes.

Saint Brigid was like the sunshine that she loved. She was warm and loving, a golden blaze of truth and purity and happiness. And she lived in a golden world, for, while Europe was being overrun by pagan invaders, Ireland remained the land of Christian learning and of Christian kings.

SAINT GENEVIEVE
GUARDIAN OF PARIS

In Paris, France, the people love Saint Genevieve, as children love a mother. Whenever their city is in danger they run to her and cry: "Help! Saint Genevieve, ask God to save us. He will listen to you!"

Three times Paris has been spared because of Saint Genevieve.

The first time was in the fifth century. Childeric, King of the Franks, and his army had surrounded the city. He intended to starve the people inside. But Saint Genevieve lived in Paris, and she had other ideas. The King she loved was far more powerful than Childeric. She asked Him what to do. He put some exciting thoughts into her head, which she put into action.

Among the starving people she found a few men who still had strength enough to walk. To them she said, "Meet me at midnight

on the side of Paris where the trees grow thick and tall beyond the city walls. I will be dressed like a man."

At midnight the men met Saint Genevieve. She told them they were to climb the city wall with her and drop over the other side, into the wood. They would land, she hoped, in a spot where there were many trees and few guards. She prayed the few would be asleep.

Light as a cricket, Genevieve was up and over the wall. The others followed. Moving like shadows, they escaped the guards and were soon in open countryside. The farmers fed them. They found boats for them, filled the boats with flour, meat, milk, eggs, and cheese. Genevieve and the men rowed the boats down-river toward Paris. Childeric's soldiers thought they were country merchants bringing food for the army. The boats were unloaded and the food inside the city before the guards discovered they had been tricked.

Another time, Attila, the Hun, and his barbarians marched on Paris. Hearing of the cruelty of these savages the people of Paris prepared to flee their city. Saint Genevieve promised them that heaven would protect Paris if they would only pray and help one another. Many people laughed at her and left. But those who stayed were glad, for Paris was untouched. Attila changed the course of his march.

Hundreds of years later an epidemic struck Paris. Thousands were dying of fever. Doctors could not cure it or keep it from spreading. The bishop asked the people to pray. But death still swept across the city. Then, remembering Genevieve, he ordered her shrine to be carried through Paris. From the moment it appeared on the streets the people began to get well. There were no new cases of the dreaded sickness. This happened in 1129, and it is called the *Miracle des Ardents*.

Genevieve Severus was born in 422 in Nantarre, a village outside Paris. She was bright and pretty and gay. She had such endearing ways that even cranky people praised her, and it is a wonder she didn't become a very spoiled little girl. She had many friends in her village among the young and old. But the One she liked best of all was Jesus. She ran into His house every day to surprise Him. Everyone knew where to look for Genevieve if they wanted her to run an errand or to play a game. She'd be in the little church, keeping Jesus company.

One day word went through the village that Germanus, the bishop, was going to preach. Genevieve was the only child who went to hear him. After the sermon the bishop asked who she was. And a villager said: "She's little Genevieve. She's a bonbon!"

"I should like to meet her," the bishop said.

When he met her he inquired: "What do you want to be when you grow up, little one?"

"A nun," she answered. He smiled and patted her head.

The next morning he gave her a medal to wear around her neck. It was the only piece of jewelry Genevieve ever wore.

There were no convents in France then. But when Genevieve grew up she began to wear plain dresses and to eat sparingly of simple food. She cared for the sick and the poor, because she thought that is what Jesus wished her to do. When her parents died she went to live with her godmother in Paris. How she loved Paris! It was so big and beautiful. There was so much for her to do. She was not there long before King Childeric's army surrounded the city and tried to starve everyone inside the walls. Then God showed everyone how much He loved Genevieve, the little girl who had always loved Him so dearly.

Saint Genevieve is the patron Saint of Paris.

SAINT GEORGE

PATRON OF ENGLAND

Years ago Christian kings and knights and soldiers tried to win the lands where Jesus had lived and died. They wanted these holy places to be protected by those who loved and believed in Him. The wars to gain these lands were called crusades.

It was on a crusade that Richard I, King of England, heard the legend of Saint George. When he and his army returned to England they talked of little else. Here is the fascinating story they told:

Saint George was a brave young Christian knight. He lived in Cappadocia, which is part of Turkey now.

Riding along alone one day, he entered the city of Sylene. The streets were empty except for one old man who crouched in a doorway. George looked around, surprised. Frightened faces stared at him from the windows of all the houses. Wonderingly, he rode up to the old man: "What goes on here, sir?" he said.

"The dragon has ruined us," the old man said. "He lives in the swamp. He breathes fire. He kills. Not even an army can get near him. We are all doomed."

"Is no one brave enough to kill the monster?" asked Saint George.

"We cannot kill him. We have tried. He destroys all who come near him. We have fed him all our sheep, all our bullocks and oxen. He is always hungry. Now, we draw lots and feed him our children! Just an hour ago the soldiers staked out the king's daughter for him. Woe! Woe unto us who have sunk so low!"

You can imagine how horrified George was when he heard this! Spurring his horse, he rode into the swamp. There he saw the princess. She was the loveliest girl he had seen in all his life. Her golden hair fell across her shoulders like a veil of sunshine. Her long soft dress was white as snow. Her eyes were blue as the sea in summertime. Butterflies fluttered all around her. She was trembling and in tears. Her arms

[104]

and legs were fastened firmly to stakes in the ground so that she could not escape the dragon.

"Fear not," George said to her. Then from the swamp emerged something so hideous he could not bear to look at it. Rising from the black ooze, writhing and terrible, he saw the dragon coming toward him. Live tongues of fire flew out of his gaping red jaws, burning the grass as he advanced. His lizardy eyes were a bright and evil green. The glittering scales that covered him jangled and grated as he moved. A smell of rot and death surrounded him.

George drove his horse forward, his lance lifted. He met the dragon on the edge of the swamp. The battle of George and the dragon filled the earth and the sky. The huge monster lashed his tail, hurling trees into the air. He snapped his mighty jaws and fire billowed to the sky. He tore the earth with his slashing claws and big stone boulders plunged at George. His eyes rolled in his head and animals scattered in terror. George used all his skill on this ugly enemy, and finally, with the last of his strength, he sent his lance into the dragon's open mouth and pinned him to the ground. While the dragon heaved and tried to loosen the lance, George freed the princess.

"Give me your sash," he said. "I will tie it around the dragon's jaws. Together we will lead him captive through the streets of the city."

"Unbolt your doors!" George shouted on the outskirts of the town. "The dragon can no longer harm you. Come and see him now!"

The king and all the people poured into the streets. Then George said to them: "Here is your dragon. Jesus gave me the strength to wound him. If you will listen to His words and promise to follow them, I will now slay the dragon for you."

They all shouted: "We will! We will!"

George plunged his lance deep into the dragon. He crumpled and died. Four huge oxcarts were needed to carry the body of the dragon into the woods.

Saint George did many brave things in his lifetime. But the bravest of all his deeds happened on the day of his death at Diospolis, in Palestine. A great persecution of Christians was going on. Many of the faithful were so frightened they were almost ready to deny their God. To strengthen their faith and give them courage, George, their knight and hero, rushed into the public square, and loudly declared his love

[105]

and belief in Christ. He was arrested, and suffered martyrdom by having his head cut off.

The people of England took Saint George to their hearts. There was something about him that suited them well. He was so young, so beautiful, so brave and good. He is the patron saint of England.

SAINT DAVID

PATRON OF WALES

Wales is a small country on the western coast of England. But it has a long history, and more mystery and riddles to it than a man could unravel in a lifetime. Crude stone tools along its coast show that men lived there 12,000 years ago. Who were they? No one knows. Men who worked with bronze tools were there 2,000 years before Christ. Who were they? Where did they come from? No one knows.

Time and dates did not matter to the Welsh. The history of their early days is all in song. And Wales, even today, is a land of poetry and music. Because of the wind, the Welshman hears music all his life. The sea wind sounds like flutes in the valley, and like harps in the mountains. The people sing along with it. Songs of lovers and villains, and of their hero, Saint David.

They will tell you Saint David was born about the year 520. His father was the prince, Sant, and his mother, the beautiful Saint Non. They say he is one of the rare ones, who gave his whole life, and not just a part of it, to God. He wanted nothing else from the beginning.

He studied the Scriptures at Vitus Rubus, which is now Henfynyw in the shire of Cardigan. There the lads in his class saw a white dove with a golden beak, "playing at his lips and teaching him to sing the praises of God." They remembered him clearly as "full of grace and lovely to behold."

David became a priest, before he felt ready to preach. So he went off to a lonely island to study with Saint Paulinus, the blind teacher. There David learned to preach wonderful sermons. He cured his teacher's blindness before he went back to the mainland of Wales, to draw souls to Jesus.

One day when he was preaching many people could neither see nor hear him. To help them the ground under David rose up to become a hill. And a snow-white dove appeared upon his shoulder. The statues of Saint David still show him as the people saw him on that day, standing on the hill with the golden-billed bird.

Crowds gathered wherever he went. People loved him and followed him. He founded twelve monasteries for them, the last one at Menevia. Here he lived with his disciples.

The people of Wales were not very good at this time. Saint David thought of ways to help them. He was very strict with his monks, and stricter with himself. When the people saw how hard they worked and how happy they were, they thought: "If David and his monks are happy with so little, how much happier we should be with so much."

When they learned that David and his monks ate only bread and vegetables and drank only water, they thought: "If they are filled with so little, we should thank God for our fine food."

When young men came to join his monastery, David made them wait ten days outside the gates. He knew the life inside was hard, and that a young Welshman would have to give up much he was used to. Only the holiest and bravest waited, and were taken in with love. The others became tired and hungry and went home.

The sweetness of David's teachings blew like a breeze across all of Wales. He became a hero to his people. It was David this, and David that. He built a great library in a day when few could write. He encouraged all forms of learning. People began to call their sons David, and prayed they would be like him.

Saint David lived to be very old. When he was dying he gave all Wales his secret. He said: "Be joyful, brothers and sisters. Keep your faith, and do the *little things* that you have seen and heard with me."

The *little things*. David knew anyone can do great things who has learned to do all little things well.

In the city of St. Davids in Pembrokeshire, Wales, you may see his empty tomb in the Cathedral. His body is not there. It may be in Glastonbury. Then again, maybe the pirates from the Orkney Islands took it. In summer, in the old days, they used to plunder Wales. But the empty tomb doesn't matter to a Welshman. They do not need his body. They have him. He is still alive and singing in their hearts.

SAINT DAVID

SAINT BENEDICT

THE RULE MAKER

Hundreds of years ago in the mountain country north of Rome there lived a powerful people called the Sabines. They are remembered for their bravery in protecting their country and the things in which they believed.

Saint Benedict was a Sabine. He was born toward the end of the fifth century to a man called Europropius and his wife, Abundantia. Cyrilla, the old nurse who cared for Benedict as a baby, later became his personal servant.

When he was about fifteen years old his parents sent him to study in Rome. He was accompanied by Cyrilla.

Rome was the capital of the world then, a great city filled with magnificent churches and palaces. The streets were thronged with people from all over the earth. Festivals, games, and parades were going on all the time. And, while life for a schoolboy in Rome was strict, there were exciting temptations all around.

Young Benedict saw those temptations leading his schoolmates away from God and their studies. He knew that someday they might lead him away, too. But before they had a chance to, he decided to leave Rome and become a monk. The faithful Cyrilla went with him. They traveled to the town of Enfide, outside Rome. Here Benedict learned all he could about the lives of monks from the priests of the Church of the Apostle Saint Peter. Here, we are told, he worked his first miracle. It happened this way: Cyrilla borrowed an earthenware sieve and accidentally broke it in two. Seeing her distress, Benedict picked up the pieces and prayed, holding them in his hands. When he rose from his knees the sieve was whole again. There was no mark to show that it had ever been broken!

This miracle drew the attention of the people to Benedict. It embarrassed him so much that he left Enfide and lived three years as a hermit in the most desolate place he could find, the site of an old mountain ruin now known as Subiaco. For clothing he wore a rough sheepskin. For food he ate wild berries and roots, and bread brought to him by a monk to whom he opened his heart.

Monks and shepherds were the first to gather round him. When he was twenty years old he was made the head of a monastery at nearby Vicovaro, much against his will as he did not feel ready for such important work. Now, as an abbot in charge of many monks, he began to see a great need for a set of firm, just rules for monks to live by. These monks, used to an easy rule and their own way, soon wished to be rid of him. He left them and returned to Subiaco, where he founded his own monastery. Hundreds of men, peasants and nobles of all ages, came from Rome to join him. For there was joy and a heavenly peace where Benedict was. Life with him attracted so many that by the time he was about fifty years old Benedict had established twelve monasteries at Subiaco. Word of his miracles, the justice of his rule, and his gentleness had spread throughout the warring and uneasy world.

Certain that his monks would carry on his work, Benedict now left Subiaco and journeyed to Monte Cassino, a mountain top eighty miles south of Rome. Here, among the marble ruins of pagan altars, he built the Abbey of Monte Cassino. Rich in experience and sanctity he now began to put his rule for monks into writing.

This rule is one of the great treasures of Christian history. It is known as the Rule of Saint Benedict. It is simple and it leads all who follow it to Heaven. Benedict wrote it to bring out the best in both ordinary and gifted men. It tells us that life is a journey to God. It divides each day into times for study, work, reading, singing, and prayer. It asks the will for obedience, order, purity, kindness, and fasting. It is a firm and reasonable road to holiness. Great men and women for more than eighteen centuries have followed it.

SAINT BERNARD

PATRON OF SKIIERS AND MOUNTAIN CLIMBERS

The little boy and his dog dug into the mound of snow on the mountainside. A head appeared. Then a man's body. The man seemed dead. Even his beard was frozen. The boy slipped a harness under his stiff arms. His dog began to drag the man through the snow. The boy ran ahead of them to the gates of his castle home high up in the mountains of the Alps. He shouted to the servants in the courtyard: "Another traveler lost in the snow! Heat blankets! Warm a mug for him!" Nearly every time the boy and his dog went out to play they found some stranger in trouble in the mountains. Either robbed or injured or lost, and often barely visible under a landslide of snow.

[114]

The time was the eleventh century. The place was a castle and its grounds near the wildest, most dangerous passes in the Alps, along the road to Rome. The little boy was Bernard, who was to become a saint.

Bernard didn't feel saintly. He didn't feel pious. He loved God, and he wanted to serve Him. He wanted to become a priest. He knew he would have to leave the mountains to do this. He would have to study a great deal. But when that was over, he could come back. He would build churches and schools in the valleys. He would join the lower peaks of the Alps with swinging bridges. He would build lookouts on the summits, and little shelters for rest at the end of difficult climbs. And on each of the two great peaks on the road to Rome he would build a hotel-hospital for tired and injured travelers. Bernard had great plans for these places, which he called hospices. He would put special monks in charge. They would be skilled in caring for the sick, the frightened, and the injured. While their bodies were healing the monks would tell them about Jesus. For many people living in remote parts of the Alps were still pagans and had never heard of Him.

This was not all of Bernard's dream. In these hospices he would breed dogs with great, strong bodies. They would have heavy fur to withstand the cold. They would have delicate noses to pick up every scrap of scent in the white wilderness of the mountains. They would be gentle and powerful. Bernard was a very ambitious boy.

When Bernard was old enough, his parents sent him to Paris to study. He boarded in a Benedictine monastery. He learned how to read and write, to hunt with hawks, and to duel with swords. He learned how to breed strong, gentle dogs with delicate noses. And the first of his many dreams came true: he was ordained a priest and sent back to his mountains.

There he built schools and churches in the valleys and swinging bridges across the lower peaks of the Alps. And on the summits of each of the two great mountain passes leading to Rome he built a hospice with a lookout station. Monks from a nearby monastery lived in them and took care of guests, the injured, and the ill. Each hospice had a kennel attached to it. Here the dogs were trained to follow human scent and rescue those lost or in trouble in the mountains. Hundreds of people were saved every year by the monks and their dogs.

The churches Bernard built brought the people the loving religion of Jesus. The schools opened the world of education to them. The bridges brought them closer together, made their travels safer, and opened the highways of trade to them. They became happier and more prosperous. All these things Bernard had dreamed. And now, through his love and labor, they had come true in his lifetime.

The two great hospices Bernard built still welcome travelers. They are called The Great Saint Bernard and The Little Saint Bernard, and are visible for miles around on their towering peaks. And the dogs that hunted for men in the snow are called Saint Bernards, after the saint who bred them for their work. Although the hospices and dogs are rarely called upon to rescue people today, they are a landmark for travelers. Thousands of tourists visit them every year.

Helicopters and airplanes are common sights in the Alps today. But before them, for many centuries there were only the hospices and the dogs of Saint Bernard to break the lonely distances and gather up the weak and the lost.

Today, visitors often take Saint Bernard puppies home with them as pets. You will find them in almost every country of the world. They are as large as little ponies, and you will often see them pulling carts with children in them.

Now the Alps are thickly settled with cities, villages, and farms. The spires of churches rise everywhere. Shrines dot the roadside. This land has become one of the favorite playgrounds of the world, and has brought riches to its people. But before Saint Bernard the country of the high Alps was white and dangerous, and only the bravest dared its cold, forbidding loneliness.

SAINT MARGARET

PATRON OF SCOTLAND

Margaret of Scotland was born in the mid-eleventh century. She was the daughter of Edward the Exile of England. In 1070 she married the handsome King Malcolm of Canmore in Scotland, and became his queen.

Margaret was a very rare person. Everyone who knew her, loved her, probably because she, herself, loved everyone. She made the right thing to do seem so pretty and pleasant that she was able to make the right thing to do quite popular.

From the day she became queen until the day she died, Margaret did both the Lord's and the world's work well in Scotland. She spread a love of Christianity among her people, while improving their manners and living conditions as well.

Margaret of Scotland had little time to herself in her lifetime as queen. She was always helping or comforting someone. She had six sons and two daughters, and all of a queen's work to do. And yet she helped found schools, abbeys, and refuges for the ill and the old. She straightened out quarrels, listened to complaints, healed broken friendships. And she is remembered as always looking fresh and welcoming and happy.

A priest who knew her well in her lifetime wrote: "So pleasant was she even in severity that all loved her, men as well as women . . ."

Saint Margaret preached her love of God and his laws with her sweet actions, rather than with words. And throughout her life she made goodness so charming that she has never been forgotten.

Margaret of Scotland died in 1093. On her deathbed she was given the saddest news of her life. Her husband, the king, and her son Edward had been murdered by the English at Alnwick! But even this heartbreaking message did not weaken her faith or her trust in the God who had made her, and whom she hoped soon to see.

Saint Margaret was buried in the church of the abbey of Dunfermline which she and her husband had founded. She was canonized a saint in 1250, and named patron of Scotland in 1673.

SAINT THOMAS BECKET

ARCHBISHOP OF CANTERBURY

At the beginning of the twelfth century, a well-to-do Norman merchant, named Becket, moved with his wife and his business from Rouen, France to London, England. Here, in 1118, a son, Thomas, was born to them. He was educated at Merton in Surrey, at the grammar school of St. Paul's Cathedral in London, and at the University of Paris.

Thomas Becket was one of the most colorful figures of his time. He was the closest and best friend of King Henry the Second of England. In their youth the two rode and hunted, dined, danced, and traveled together in the rich, courtly circles of royal England. They were both worldly, strong, popular, hot-tempered, and handsome men. These good companions seemed inseparable.

Thomas Becket would stand out in any age, in any country. He was an exciting person in appearance and in accomplishment. Even after he studied Church Law at Bologna in Italy, and was made archdeacon of Canterbury Cathedral in 1154, he behaved much more like a prince than a man on his way to the priesthood. He deferred only to his friend, the king. And Henry the Second had a right to feel that he held this fellow in the hollow of his hand, that of all people Thomas Becket would never oppose him.

In 1155 the king appointed him Lord Chancellor of England. He now held two high offices: one for his God, and one for his country. He was only thirty-seven years old. And then, on June 2, 1162, Thomas Becket was ordained a priest and made Archbishop of Canterbury.

The formal vestments of an archbishop include a shepherd's crook, or staff. This is to remind all who hold this sacred office that they are now shepherds, in charge of a flock, and accountable to God for every member of that flock.

Thrilled and shaken at the responsibility of this office, Thomas Becket took the staff in his hands. Begging God's help, he promised to do all in his power, to give up his life if need be, in defense of his flock. He knew that to do this meant giving up all the earthly things he loved: the bay of hounds in the woods of the hunt, the company of knights in the royal banquet halls, the long, lovely, agreeable days of worldly power and sport, the close companionship of his friend, Henry, King of England. In a sublime moment, full of grace, he offered himself and all that he loved on earth to God. He resigned as Chancellor of England!

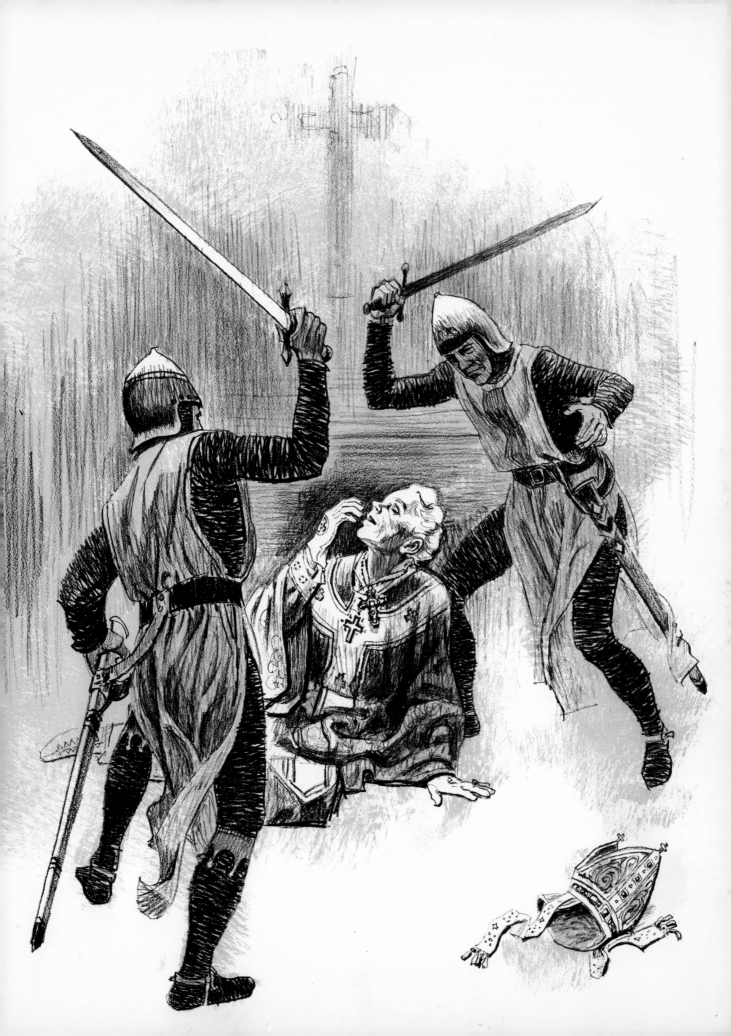

When King Henry saw that Thomas was taking this new church honor so seriously, he became very angry. He missed the old, close companionship. His anger increased as he found Thomas opposing him whenever he interfered with the liberties of the people or the rights of the church. They quarreled. Their quarrels became frequent and more violent. The old friendship weakened. Thomas thought a separation might help. He went to France.

He returned to England on December 1, 1170, to continue his friendship with Henry. He hoped the king now realized that his glory lay in giving the people and the church more, and not less liberty, in their affairs. This the king was not prepared to do. Thomas argued for justice, the king for more power. Stung because Thomas was standing with the people and with the church against him, the king became angry.

Impulsively he complained of Thomas to his knights. "Have I not about me one man of enough spirit to rid me of a single insolent prelate?" he said.

The knights took this as an order.

On the evening of December 29, 1170, four of the king's knights murdered Thomas Becket in Canterbury Cathedral! All England was outraged! When news of his death reached King Henry he was heart-broken. They had indeed quarreled bitterly. But the king loved Thomas as a brother, nevertheless. And there was no one on earth he had admired as much. That a rash remark of his had caused his murder was a torture to him. And a further torment was the fury of the people, who blamed him for the archbishop's death. He shut himself away from everyone, fasted and wept for forty days, as a self-inflicted penance. Then as an atonement gift the living Thomas would have loved, King Henry founded in his dead friend's honor the first house of Carthusian monks in England. Saint Hugh of Lincoln was the abbot.

After the death of Thomas Becket unknown qualities of this proud man were discovered. As his broken body was lifted from the cathedral floor he was seen to be wearing a prickly hair shirt under his elegant robes. Others were found in his room. The poor told of his endless, quiet giving. And those close to him said he walked in innocence among temptations as great as any man has ever been asked to endure.

Thomas Becket was canonized immediately after his death.

SAINT HUGH
OF LINCOLN
THE LEPERS' FRIEND

Early in the twelfth century a wealthy young lord, named William, made his decision to become a knight instead of a monk. He fought bravely in many wars and married a lovely lady, Anne. They lived in the castle of Avalon in the province of Burgundy in France, and there three sons were born to them. When Hugh, the youngest, was eight years old his mother died, and the longing to become a monk returned to his father. William then divided his fortune among his sons and entered a monastery, taking young Hugh with him.

The boy was raised and educated by the monks. He knew no other life except one devoted to God from that time on. His playmates were the animals of the forest. They came when he called them, curled up in his arms, and ate from his hand.

Hugh, too, became a monk and a priest. He joined a very strict order, the Carthusians, and until he was forty years old he was attached to a monastery in southern France called the Grande Chartreuse.

At this time King Henry II of England promised to build monasteries in Britain in honor of Thomas Becket, Archbishop of Canterbury. This promise was in addition to the public penance he had already performed for his part in the murder of Thomas, his friend. Hugh was sent from France to found the monastery at Witham, in Somerset. He at once became immensely popular with the people of the countryside.

Six years later and much against his will he was appointed Bishop of Lincoln. Word of his holiness and his wisdom spread over England. He loved the people. He was particularly kind to the sick, the needy, and the oppressed. In return they opened their hearts to him.

One day walking through an English forest he heard the ringing of little bells. He moved toward the sweet sound and heard a voice crying: "Unclean! Unclean!"

He heard the cry again. It was the saddest sound. Turning, he saw

[125]

a man. Or was it a man, this poor, earth-colored heap before him? The man's face was dirty and disfigured. The hand that held the bell had only parts of fingers. The eyes lifted to his held only fright and loneliness.

As Hugh rushed toward him the bell rang faster than ever and the man cried out again: "Unclean! I am a leper!"

Bishop Hugh was not afraid of leprosy.

"My brother!" he whispered, lifting the man into his arms.

He held water from a nearby spring to the cracked lips. He bathed the poor body and put his sandals on the leper's feet. Then he made a bed of twigs for him and softened it with his cloak.

Bishop Hugh visited all the bell ringers in the forest that day. When he went back to the city of Lincoln he made his people feel ashamed of the way they had treated these unfortunates. He urged them to build hospitals and to find out how people contracted this terrible disease. Soon, under his guidance, the hospitals were built. Lepers were no longer condemned to live and die in the woods like animals, and before long this dread sickness vanished from England.

In pictures and statues Hugh is shown with a swan. And the reason for this is that a fierce wild swan once attached itself to him. It would fly to his house before his return from a mission and await his arrival on the roof. It would stand guard while he slept, eat bread from his hand, and dive its head and long neck into the wide sleeves of his habit. And in the springtime mother birds would bring their young for him to admire, lining them up on his window sill.

Although as bishop Hugh held a princely office, he always followed the strict order of his rule. He ate the simplest food and wore the rough habit of the Carthusians. And every morning upon waking, it is said, he prayed: "Lord Jesus, help me this day to act as You would, if You were here!"

Bishop Hugh of Lincoln died on November 16, 1200. He was buried in the Cathedral of Lincoln on November 24. It was a day of universal grief. Packed into the cathedral and spilling out all over the city were

those whom he had loved, served, and defended. Two kings and their retinues knelt with bowed heads in the cathedral that day: King John of England, and William the Lion of Scotland. In the sanctuary there were three archbishops, the primate of England, and one hundred

abbots. The Jews from the ghetto of Lincoln were there too, bewailing the loss of the great loving servant of God who had protected them from persecution and defended them from the violence of mobs. Hugh was canonized a saint in the year 1220.

SAINT ISIDORE

PATRON OF MADRID

In the twelfth century in Madrid, the capital of Spain, a little boy called Isidore was born. He came into this world in the ugly section of the city where the poor, the beggars, and the gypsies lived. He was a plain little boy, small and thin, with dark eyes and wispy black hair. He never went to school at all, because his parents could not afford to send him. Often they could not even feed him. But they gave him two great gifts in his childhood that he kept with him all his life: a love of prayer and a hatred of sin.

While Isidore was still in his mother's arms she took him to the only palace he ever visited. This was the church that rose like a castle above the tumble-down houses of the poor. It became Isidore's second home throughout his life. Here the image of Jesus on the Cross welcomed him with a sad, sweet smile. The Jesus who was God, and yet who had been as poor as Isidore when He lived on earth. The Jesus who loved him so much He wanted him to live with Him in the palace of the Kingdom of Heaven. And surrounding Him stood the statues of the saints. God must be so proud of them, Isidore thought. Maybe, if he did the best he could every day, and asked Jesus to help him, he could become a saint, too. Not a great one as the statue saints were, but a small secret one that only God knew about.

Isidore was still a little boy when he had to leave home and go to work. A wealthy Spaniard, John de Vergas, made him a laborer in his fields.

Isidore had often been hungry. Now that he had big, farm meals to fill out his bony young body he found he could not enjoy them. For there were always beggars standing hopefully at the farm gates at mealtime, working their tongues across their lips. The sight of them took Isidore's appetite away. He shared his meals with them, and after they had eaten, the scraps they left tasted like feasts to Isidore. The

other workmen called him a fool. Each morning before his long work-day he went to church. All day, as he guided the plow through the fields, thoughts of God and His creation filled his mind. The years rolled on and Isidore grew into manhood.

He married a girl as poor and as good as himself. Otherwise his life did not change. He remained a laborer on the farm of John de Vergas all of his life. The fields he tended were the best cared for and bore the richest harvest. We are told that because of this the other workers complained. They said that going to church made Isidore late for work every morning. John de Vergas watched to see if this were true. It was. Angered, he rode into Isidore's field to scold him. But as he drew near he saw a second team of snow-white oxen being led by tall, shadowy strangers! They were plowing beside the team driven by Isidore. Humbled, he turned away from the quiet little man whom Heaven was helping. Others told of having seen angels working in his field with him.

Another time, legend tells us, Isidore was carrying grain to the mill to be ground into flour. It was a cold winter day and birds drooped on tree branches for lack of food. Isidore opened his sack and poured half the grain on the ground for them. His companions laughed at him, and said he would be punished for this waste. But when they reached the mill Isidore's sack was full of grain. And when it was ground it gave twice as much flour as other sacks of the same size and weight.

Saint Isidore died on May 15, 1130. Spain is full of legends about his life and miracles. He never met anyone as great as a king in his lifetime. Yet he served the kings of Spain well after his death. When Alfonso of Castile was fighting the Moors in 1211 it is said that Isidore showed him a secret path in a dream, by which he was able to surprise and defeat the enemy. Four hundred years later King Philip III of Spain was ill and dying. The shrine of Isidore was carried from the Church of Saint Andrew in Madrid to the king's sickroom. At the hour it left the church the fever left the king, and when the shrine entered his room, he recovered completely.

[132] Isidore was canonized in March 1622, and is the patron of the city of Madrid. Today his statue stands in the churches of Spain among those saints he admired so much as a little boy.

SAINT FRANCIS OF ASSISI

THE BEGGAR SAINT

This is the story of Saint Francis of Assisi, one of the most beloved saints who ever lived.

He was a thin, little, starved-looking clown of a man, not at all handsome, and he often rushed into things without thinking. He loved candy and desserts, but he lived on the crusts of beggars. And he made up and sang the most beautiful songs. And he died, singing.

In his lifetime he learned to love God and all His creation so much that his love became as catching as laughter and filled the world around him. Rich man, poor man, beggar man, thief, doctor, lawyer, merchant, chief, flocked to him, and they still do. He founded an order of monks, called the Franciscans, and an order of nuns, called the Poor Clares. He called Sun, Wind, Fire, and Wolves, his Brothers; Earth, his Mother; Water, Moon and Stars, and Death, his Sisters; Poverty, a Lady. He was gentle as a lamb, the Little Singer of God.

Saint Francis of Assisi was born to Pietro and Pica de Bernardone in Assisi, Italy, in 1181. At his christening in the church of San Rufino he was called John. But his father admired everything French, and he called his eldest son, "The Little Frenchman." Soon everyone forgot his given name, and he became known to all as Francis de Bernardone.

The Bernardone family was very rich. Young Francis wore elegant clothes covered with costly braids and embroideries, and he ate only the finest of foods. He was very popular and liked a good time, and he could always be found at the center of the merrymaking at parties, dances, and games, and wherever interesting and exciting things were going on. His father kept his pockets filled with golden ducats, and Francis tossed them away on anything that pleased his fancy.

But one night, coming home from a party when he was twenty-two years old, Francis fell behind his gay crowd of friends, and soon found himself alone on one of Assisi's crooked, darkened streets. He looked up at the sky and saw its dusky perfection lighted with the shining order of the stars. There, alone in the stillness of the night, he was filled with a peace and sweetness he had never known before. He felt close to God. He was suddenly weary of the parties and the play that always have to end in tiredness and in loneliness. He felt wasted and empty and useless against the big beauty of God's night. For the night wouldn't wrinkle and soil as his fine clothes would. The cakes and wine he had eaten only made him feel uncomfortable, now. And the gold in his pockets could never buy even one small piece of such a sky. How great is God! he thought. He began to pray. And as he did the saint in him began to grow.

The next day he found an old tumbledown chapel, where, hidden from all but God, he could look at his Saviour on the Crucifix, and ask Him what to do with his life. And one day in this neglected chapel of San Damiano, God gave him His answer: "Now go hence, Francis, and build up My church, for it is falling down."

From that day on Francis became a Beggar of the Lord. He repaired

the little chapel of San Damiano with his own hands. He lived in a cave, begged for his food, and wore a rough, brown woolen garment belted with rope. He preached and sang the love of God into the hearts of men and birds and beasts. He loved Christ his Saviour so much that he even wanted to feel like Him, when He was dying on the Cross. And before he died God gave him that feeling, too. He marked his little body with the wounds of the crucifixion. And so, at last, Saint Francis of Assisi came as near as a man can to the image of Jesus, when He walked the earth, suffered, and died for us.

SAINT DOMINIC

FOUNDER OF THE ORDER OF PREACHERS

When Dominic lived he was loved by thousands. He was a man of great learning, charming, easy to know. Since his death he has been admired and respected as a great saint. But he has never been as loved and popular as he deserves to be. Not many baby boys are named for him. Not many turn to him in time of trouble or joy. This wonderful saint is hidden almost completely behind the great things he did. To find him we have to go back to the end of the twelfth century in Spain, when he was a little boy.

Dominic was the third son of Felix Guzman and his wife, Joanna of Aza. He was born about 1170 in Calaruega, Spain. By then his parents were no longer young. His two brothers were grown men and gone from home: Antony, a priest, and Mannes, a monk.

Born into a family that had already given two sons to the church, Dominic was surrounded by the same teaching and example that had turned his brothers toward God. We know that he played "monk" as children today play cowboy. And this is the one picture we have of him as a child: a little boy wandering through a quiet house dressed as a monk and copying the speech and gestures of every monastic he had ever known or seen!

We next hear of Dominic when he entered the University of Palencia in Spain at fourteen. He was far younger than the other students, and this must have set him apart from them—in all but learning. Not until he had completed four years at the University was he allowed to begin the studies that ended in his ordination to the priesthood.

He then joined a group of monks in charge of the cathedral at Osma, Spain. We know that while there, he slept on the floor, refused wine with his meals, and sold his library to feed the poor. These books were great treasures to Dominic. They were written by hand on parchment made from the stretched skins of animals, for printing had not

been invented; few people could afford books in those days. Yet Dominic parted with his gladly, saying: "But I could not bear to prize dead skins when living skins were starving and in want." During this time he even tried to sell *himself!* He offered to become a slave so that a frightened captive of the Moors could go free.

In 1204 Dominic's life changed suddenly. Alfonso IX, King of Castile, chose the Bishop of Osma to travel to Denmark and arrange a marriage for his son, Ferdinand. The bishop took Dominic with him.

The travelers rested at Languedoc in France. There they were horrified to discover that a false doctrine was spreading over this Christian country. When the bishop completed his mission he left Dominic in France to fight this heresy with truth. This became his life work. Dominic now gathered a group of learned and appealing men around him, gave them a rule, and founded the Order of Preachers, the Dominican friars.

These friars did not remain in a monastery with him, but were sent to preach true Christianity all over Europe. He established at about the same time the first convent of Dominican nuns, all of whom were noblewomen and converts.

Dominic established sixty friaries in fifteen years. Whenever it was possible these were associated with each country's great seats of learning: in France, near the University of Paris; in Italy, close by the University of Bologna; in England, at Oxford, Cambridge, and London.

Learning, study of the Bible, teaching, and preaching were from the beginning of first importance in his order.

There is a story told about Dominic's meeting with Francis of Assisi. In a vision he saw the Mother of God pointing out two figures to her Son. One of them, Dominic knew, was himself, but the other one was a stranger. Next day in a Roman church he saw a ragged little beggar, and recognized him as the stranger. Going up to him he embraced him and said: "You are my companion and must walk with me. For if we hold together no earthly power can withstand us." This meeting of the founders of the Dominican and Franciscan orders is still celebrated twice each year, when priests of the two orders sing Mass in each other's churches.

Dominic died on August 6, 1221. He was about fifty-one years old. He was canonized in 1234.

SAINT BÉNEZET

THE BRIDGEBUILDER

Bénezet was a poor little shepherd boy of the twelfth century who tended his widowed mother's sheep in a meadow beside the Rhone River in France. He was a quiet little Christian, and his work gave him much time to think. With the blue sky above him, the river beside him, wild flowers at this feet, and the peaks of the Alps in the distance, Bénezet had a fine view of God's creation.

Because we cannot see God, all of us form pictures of Him in our hearts. Bénezet saw Him as a master builder, a shaper of mountains and rivers, the maker of man and animals, birds and fishes. Then he would look from the landscape around him to his own rough, unskilled hands. What could they do to praise God except simple, heavy work? And his mind was as rough as his hands. He could not read or write. Listening and watching were his only teachers. His speech was as rough as his hands and mind, so he had best be still and not try to praise God with that, either. But love for God—that he had such a plenty of that he longed for a way to show it that would take all of his strength, all of his time.

Often Bénezet would look out upon the Rhone River rushing on its way from Lake Geneva to the Mediterranean Sea. How difficult it was for people to cross it, Bénezet thought. How frightened people were of it, and how often they drowned! But he could not help them except with prayers whenever he saw them leave the shore.

One day during an eclipse of the sun he heard, or dreamed he heard, a voice calling him. It told him to go to Avignon and build a bridge over the river rapids of the Rhone!

In the Middle Ages the building and repairing of bridges was considered a work of mercy. Rich men often gave money for this work, or left funds for it in their wills. But Bénezet was poor and ignorant and very small for his age. He knew nothing at all about bridges.

[139]

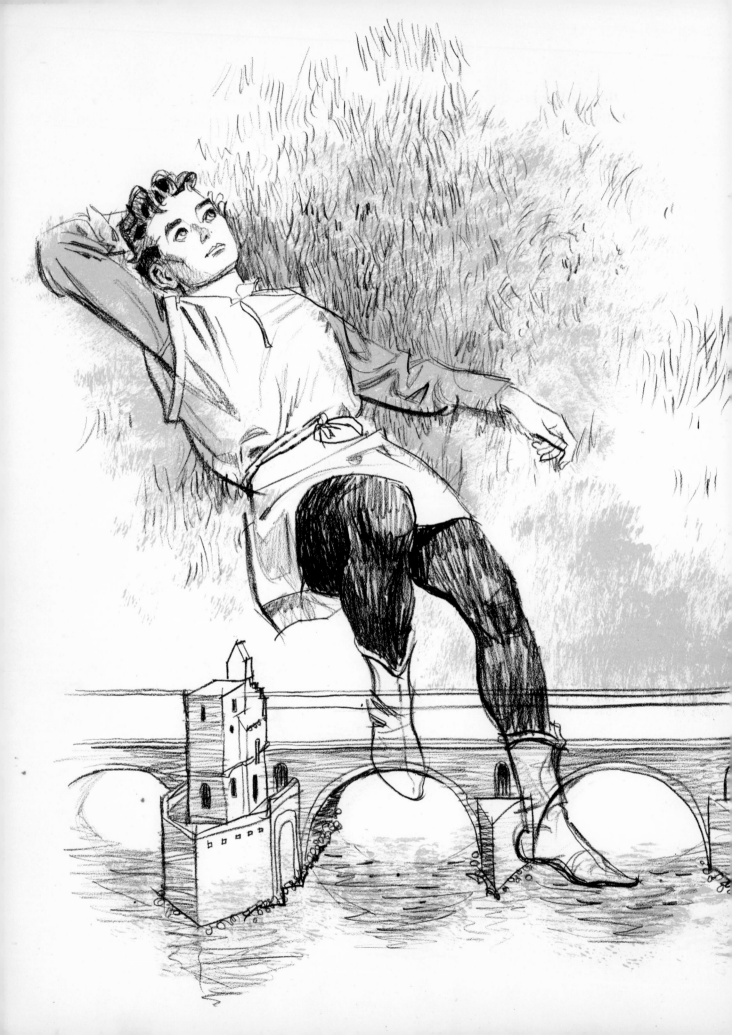

But the dream, the vision, was too real to be denied. He obeyed it, gladly. He went to Avignon and told the bishop he had come to build a bridge across the rapids of the Rhone. At first the bishop thought he was joking, but a miracle we know nothing about took place, and caused him to give Bénezet permission to build a stone bridge where none had ever been before. It was a dangerous undertaking. The work began in 1177.

For seven years little Bénezet directed all building operations and worked from sunup to sundown on the bridge. By 1184 all the main difficulties had been overcome, the dangerous work completed. Bénezet died that year and his worn little body was buried on the bridge. The wonders which surrounded the building of this bridge and the miracles at Bénezet's grave convinced the people of Avignon that a chapel should be erected on the bridge to hold Bénezet's tomb. His body lay in this shrine for five hundred years. In 1669, when part of the bridge was washed away, Bénezet's coffin was recovered from the Rhone. It was opened the following year, and his body was found to be as clean and pure and sound as on the day he died. Saint Bénezet is one of the patron saints of Avignon. In English he is called Little Benedict the Bridgebuilder.

SAINT HEDWIG

THE DUCHESS

Hedwig, or Jadwiga, as she is sometimes called, was the daughter of the German Count and Countess Berthold. She was born in Bavaria about the year 1174, and educated at a monastery boarding school. While still in her teens she married Henry, young son of the Duke of Silesia. (Today most of Silesia is in southwestern Poland.)

The people were strong and hard-working. The land was rich in minerals and grew fine farm crops. It was a Christian country, but it needed schools, libraries, churches, and hospitals, and educated people to operate them.

Henry and Hedwig had seven children and a burning ambition to see Christianity and knowledge flourish in their land. In 1202 Henry became Duke of Silesia. This deeply religious couple now had the wealth and position necessary to carry out their desires.

Henry began at once to build the first convent for women in Silesia, the Cistercian convent at Trebnitz. All criminals sentenced for evil-doing worked on this building. One after another they built monasteries all over Silesia for monks of the Augustinian, Dominican, Franciscan, and Cistercian orders. Henry established a hospital in Breslau, the capital, and Hedwig built one for women lepers at Neumarkt. Christian and German culture began to spread across Silesia. Everything the duke and duchess established was successful. It looked as though their lives were charmed. But no life is lived without some sorrow, and theirs came from the place where it hurt them most: from their children. Only one of them, Gertrude, was alive at her mother's death. The others quarreled among themselves over property, or were killed in wars.

Hedwig often retired to the Trebnitz convent. Humbly she took part in the strict exercises of the Cistercian nuns. As a penance she often went to church barefoot over ice and snow. After her husband's death she wore the habit of the Cistercian sisters and used her fortune for the relief of her needy countrymen.

Many legends have been written about Hedwig. It is said that she performed marvelous miracles in her lifetime. Wealth to her was useful only to spread the honor and glory of God. And for this she used it all of her lifetime.

Hedwig, Duchess of Silesia, died in October 1243. She was buried in the convent at Trebnitz which her husband had founded, and in which her daughter, Gertrude, was abbess. Hedwig was canonized in 1267.

SAINT CLARE

THE LITTLE LIGHT OF ASSISI

"Faverone, isn't she beautiful?"

"She will be lovely as you are, someday, Ortolana."

"She has your wonderful eyes, Faverone."

"And your golden hair. The light of the sun is in it."

"Then, let us call her 'Clare', our little light."

It was the year 1194. In the nursery of a noble house in Assisi, Italy, the young Offreduccios were looking at their first baby. Everything around this new little girl was luxurious. Her cradle was inlaid with gold. Her coverlets were silk and softest wool.

Assisi was a most important trade center in Italy in those days. Picture-book houses lined its narrow, hilly streets. Jugglers performed on its squares. Knights in armor rode by. Donkeys wore garlands and bells as they pulled farm carts into town. This was Clare's city. Here she learned to read and write, to sing and dance, sew and embroider. Here people turned to look at the Offreduccio girl who grew more beautiful each day. She was the dream of all the town's young nobles.

In her teens Clare often thought of marriage. But none of the young men in Assisi appealed to her. There must be someone, somewhere, she thought, whom she could love with all her heart. She became restless and uneasy. This happens to all of us. And most young Christians do what Clare did. They ask God to help them, to give them a little sign. Here is the way He helped Clare:

Francis Bernardone, whom the world knows today as Saint Francis of Assisi, was giving a sermon in a nearby church. Clare and her father went to hear him, for he was said to thrill his listeners. Once he had been as rich as Clare, reckless and pleasure-loving. Now he was a monk and a beggar, and the happiest person Clare had ever seen.

Francis talked about poverty. He said Jesus loved those who gave up everything to follow Him. He said living for Jesus was the most exciting adventure on earth. And he looked as if it were. He was just a little bundle of bones in a ragged habit. But above the shabby robe his eyes twinkled and his face was radiant with a secret joy.

Clare felt that Christ had spoken to her through Francis. She was sure He was asking her to follow Him. She knew her family would object. She remembered hearing that Francis's father had thought him crazy to go off and become a barefoot monk.

After the sermon Clare talked to Francis about herself. He said he thought that Jesus must want her very much, for Himself, or she would not be filled with such happiness at the thought of living for Him alone.

On Monday, March 19, 1212, Clare eloped! Through the dark streets she ran to meet her bridegroom. But it was Jesus she was running to-

ward, and no earthly lover. And it was straight toward Him she ran all her life.

Francis met her at the chapel of Our Lady of the Angels outside Assisi. At the altar she exchanged her lovely dress for a coarse wool robe. She tied a knotted rope around her waist, and traded her jeweled slippers for rough sandals. Francis cut off her golden hair. Then Clare took the three vows of poverty, chastity, and obedience to her Eternal Lover. Immediately Francis took her to the Sisters' Convent of Saint Paul, where she was welcomed and sheltered.

Her family was furious. They came to the convent to take her home. But Clare would not leave. Soon her sister Agnes joined her. Francis built a little convent for them. He made rules for prayer and work and the sisters lived by them. Later Clare was joined by her mother and many friends. Each gave up everything she possessed, and most of them possessed a great deal of worldly wealth.

Because no one in the convent had any money, some of the nuns had to beg each day. This is how they became known as the Poor Clares. Every day was an adventure. They never knew what they were going to eat. Or where they would get cloth, candles, or fuel. They had no beds. They ate no meat. They worked terribly hard, gardening, caring for the poor and sick, scrubbing, cooking, sewing.

Clare made a rule of her own for her sisters. They could do no unnecessary talking. Gossip never entered her convent. But there was no law against smiling. No law against joy. Women flocked to her. She founded convents in Italy, France, Germany, and Bohemia.

Clare always did the hardest work. She washed and kissed the tired feet of her begging sisters. She served at table, and she prayed while they slept. And once, when an army threatened Assisi, she prayed it away.

Just before her death Clare was too weak to attend Christmas Mass in the church. But from her poor convent room she seemed to see and hear it all. She followed the Mass, just as if she had been there. From this ability to see something clearly that was beyond the range of her eyes, Saint Clare has been named the patron of television.

Saint Clare was fifty-nine years old when she died, and her last words on earth were: "Blessed be Thou, O God, for having created me."

Only the happiest people say such things about life. Clare was canonized in 1255.

SAINT ALBERT THE GREAT

PATRON OF SCIENTISTS

Albert was born about 1206 to the Count and Countess of Bollstädt in the castle of Lauingen on the River Danube, in what today is southern Germany.

It was in the deep, beautiful forest around Lauingen that Albert became familiar with the animals, plants, and insects that interested him all his life. From early childhood he loved the outdoors and all living creatures. While still very young he became an expert in the handling of hawks, dogs, and horses.

Albert grew into a young man of great strength, ability, and determination. At seventeen he entered the University of Padua in Italy to become a scientist. There many of his teachers were Dominican monks. These monks were the first people he had ever met who combined worldly and divine wisdom in their lives. They fascinated him. He wanted to become one of them. But his family objected. They felt that as a Dominican his rank and ability would be wasted. Over their strong objections Albert entered the Order. He was not quite sure of himself when he did this. Giving up his wealth and nobility troubled him, too. Carrying on his scientific studies as he wished meant much to him. Placing his mind under the direction of a superior was almost unthinkable. The idea of doing everything his own way was so strong that he almost gave up Dominican life. Bending his will to his superior's was a mighty sacrifice for Albert. But bend it he did.

When his studies were completed at Padua he was sent to Paris to take his Doctorate in Theology. From there he was sent to teach at the University of Cologne. Here, shy, young Thomas of Aquino, who was to become Saint Thomas Aquinas, became his pupil, and their lifelong friendship began. Albert's fame grew. Soon he was placed in charge of all Dominicans in Germany, Austria, and Serbia. He crossed this large province many times, always on foot. Wherever he went he would observe animal and plant life in woods, on the mountains and in the plains. These were happy years for him. But it was not long before he was back in Paris teaching at the University, the most distinguished seat of learning in Europe at that time. From there he was sent all over Europe, preaching, teaching, organizing. But he was not teaching or preaching science. He was preaching and teaching Christianity. Naturally science crept in, because it is one of the things that spins endlessly from God's creation. By itself, it is accurate and cold, without pity and without love. But as one of the splendid gifts of God it becomes a warm and powerful aid to all mankind: science comforts and makes life happier, healthier, and more convenient. Albert loved it more than ever as it unfolded under God, and he composed it as other men compose music or paintings.

Albert's writing on science gave no new rules, except this important one: insistence on proof. He produced many true and accurate observations. No one had ever studied insects or spiders before. He was the first man in fifteen hundred years to consider the use and scientific function of plants. He wrote down the habits of the beaver, deer, elk, bison, otter, marten, ferret, skunk, brown bear and Polar bear, eagle, and crocodile. He recorded the properties of minerals. He, who reluctantly gave up a life of science for a life of God, left to us more new observations of science than any man of his time.

Albert was his name. But because of his fame as a teacher he was known all over Europe in his lifetime as Albertus Magnus, or Albert the Great.

Old and beloved, he died peacefully at Cologne in Germany on November 15, 1280. He was canonized on December 16, 1931.

SAINT LOUIS IX

THE KING OF FRANCE

The palace was strangely quiet as the handsome boy and his servant rode into the courtyard. They leaped from their horses laughing, but their high spirits ended abruptly. The bells in the tower began to toll. As the big bronze tongues struck, the faces in the courtyard paled. The hawk on the boy's shoulder shuddered. Bolts of black cloth were being draped over the king's standard. The bells were tolling the death dirge of Louis VIII, King of France. The boy in the courtyard was his son, Prince Louis.

In the year 1214 the Capet family had ruled France for more than two hundred years. Under these Christian kings the country had grown from a few scattered villages around Paris to almost the size it is today. It was the richest and most powerful country in Europe. The time in history called the Middle Ages was almost over. Louis VIII was King of France, and Blanche of Castile, his wife, was Queen. On April 25, at Poissy, their first child, the Prince Louis, was born.

From early childhood this boy knew that someday he would be king. He had been trained by word and example to love God above all things, and to find his wisdom in the ways and teachings of Jesus.

The day the bells tolled Prince Louis was twelve years old. He was now crowned Louis IX, King of France, with his mother as Regent. His childhood was over. He was severely disciplined and never allowed to forget that much was expected of him. He married at nineteen, and the kingdom was turned over to him when he came of age in 1235.

From the day Louis became King of France until the day he died, he tried to administer his country as if God, Himself, were ruling it— with justice and generosity and love. He set out to make all of France a song of beauty and praise to the One who had created it.

He began his reign by showing a special concern for the poor and the old. He built hospitals and places of refuge and comfort for them.

He took them into his palaces, clothed and fed them from his personal stores. And on each Holy Thursday he had beggars brought to him, so that, like Christ, he could wash their feet with his hands.

This king cast his lot with his people rather than with the nobles. Under him merchants, printers, weavers, carpenters, artisans in stone, metal, and paint formed special groups called guilds. In these they learned from each other and taught their trades to young workmen. Through the guilds they could protect their interests, advance their talents, and gain greater respect for their work and themselves. Each tried to outdo the other, and many a masterpiece was the result. As their skill improved so did their happiness and their earnings and opportunities. France became a pleasanter place in which to live. A new form of building flourished. It was called Gothic. All over France new cathedrals began to rise with slender stone spires that seemed to pierce the sky.

Louis IX lived to see his nobles mingling with the workingmen, building the great cathedrals. As the huge blocks of stone were drawn from the quarries, history tells us: ". . . gentry and peasants alike had the cords attached to their arms, chests, and shoulders and drew the loads along like beasts of burden."

Under his guidance and encouragement magnificent roads, bridges, and homes appeared; the famous vineyards of France were planted on the dry, sunny hills, the cattle fattened on the plains, and the harvests grew great. With this bounty the cooks of France began to earn a fame that ever since has been theirs.

Under him a fine university rose in Paris, the Sorbonne. Here he hoped good minds could be trained to greatness in the arts and sciences, knowledge from all over the world could be shared and spread.

Louis IX led two crusades. He longed, like many before him, to see the Holy Land in Christian hands. But he was not granted this wish. On his first crusade he was captured by the Moslems, held for ransom, and tortured because he would not renounce his faith. His proud bearing and his loyalty to his beliefs gained him the admiration of his captors. He was ransomed for the return of their city, Diametta in Egypt, which was then held by his army. On the other crusade he caught the plague and died in Tunis in Africa in 1270.

Just before he died, he who had worn the crown and ermine of the

Capet kings asked to be placed upon a bed of ashes on the ground. This was reluctantly done by those who loved him. Stripped of every sign of royalty, he folded his arms peacefully across his breast, closed his eyes, and went like a beggar to his God, murmuring "Jerusalem! Jerusalem!"

He was canonized in 1297.

SAINT THOMAS AQUINAS

THE "GIANT" SAINT

In the year 1225, in the mountain castle of Rocca Secca above the town of Aquino, in Italy, the seventh child of the knight, Count Landulf of Aquino and his Norman wife, Theodora, was born. He was named Thomas.

On a high hill a few miles to the south of his father's castle stood the great Abbey of Monte Cassino. Its abbot, Landulf Sinibaldo, was a kinsman of the Aquino family. From the time he was five until he was almost thirteen he lived and went to school in this famous monastery. A few days after his arrival, little Thomas faced the abbot with this question: "What is God?" The answer to this question was to consume his life.

This boy, the son of nobles and cousin of the Holy Roman Emperor, Frederick II, might easily have led the life of luxury that was the pattern of his kind in those days. Instead, he chose the study of God and, in so doing, Thomas Aquinas gave to the world a precious gift of knowledge.

By the time he entered the University of Naples, Thomas had grown into a young giant. In appearance he was more Norman than Italian. He was fair-skinned and very tall. His big-boned body was fully fleshed and powerful. His hands and feet and head were huge. Under broad brows his eyes gazed out upon the world, brilliant, thoughtful, and compassionate. He had strength enough, even as a young man, to break smaller men as if they were matchsticks, yet he never laid a violent hand on any living thing. Extremely shy, modest, and quiet, Thomas was a gentle giant.

[156] Much more important than his physical greatness was his giant intellect. In that head such thoughts were bobbing as would light the Christian world forever!

While in Naples, Thomas attended the Dominican Church, and soon became attracted to the life of the Order of Preachers. So attracted was he that before he had quite completed his university studies he joined the Dominican Begging Friars. His family were infuriated. Believing that Thomas could be persuaded to follow a life in keeping with their noble position, his elder brothers kidnaped him and locked him in a room in the Aquino castle. Here Thomas remained for two years. Far from changing his mind, imprisonment strengthened it. During this time he memorized most of the Bible and wrote his first paper on the errors of the famous Greek teacher, Aristotle, whom he greatly admired.

Finally, with the aid of one of his sisters, Thomas escaped his prison and rejoined his brother Dominicans. They sent him to Paris and then Cologne to study under Albertus Magnus, the most famous professor of his time.

Day after day Thomas sat in his classes, his huge body hunched in his chair, his mind absorbed in thought. The other students were anxious to be heard, but Thomas sat silently. Soon he was nicknamed, "The Dumb Sicilian Ox." One day a student, moved to pity for this big, seemingly stupid fellow, began to explain a difficult lesson to him. He listened gratefully to the point where the helpful student could go no further. Then Thomas astounded him by finishing the difficult part of the lesson for him.

Albertus Magnus, the Dominican teacher, was not misled by the shyness and silence of Thomas. He gave him a most difficult public test. The gentle giant's answers astonished even his teacher. They showed knowledge and understanding of the highest order. Under him the mind and heart of Thomas opened and exposed their wonder. Neither dreamed it at the time, but in that classroom a saint was teaching a saint.

Thomas was ordained a priest. At the suggestion of Albertus Magnus he was sent to the University of Paris where he mingled with great minds of the medieval world—Saint Bonaventure and Roger Bacon. There he sat at table before a king who would also become a saint— Louis IX of France. And there he became known as one of the greatest Christian teachers the world has ever known.

Thomas was a poet, an artist, a philosopher, and a musician. Among scholars his *Summa theologiae* is considered the fullest exposition of theological teaching ever given the world. But he is remembered by most of us for his beloved church hymns: "O salutaris" and "Tantum ergo," the familiar Benediction songs.

Saint Thomas Aquinas is known among scholars as the philosopher who combined Aristotelian and Christian wisdom to show that religious faith and human reason are partners, and not enemies. It is this very greatness of his that has kept us from knowing him better. For, standing in awe of his work, we forget that to be great he had to have within him more love, more understanding, more compassion and sweetness than most.

Saint Thomas Aquinas is called the "Light of the Christian Church" and the "Angelic Doctor." He died on the seventh of March in the year 1274 in the Cistercian Monastery of Fossa Nuova, in Italy. He was canonized in 1323, forty-nine years after his death. His body lies in the Cathedral of Saint-Sernin in Toulouse, France, where it was brought from Italy by the Begging Friars he had joined in his youth. It is not surprising that brilliant, lovable, humble Thomas is the patron saint of colleges, universities, and schools.

SAINT ZITA

PATRON OF SERVANTS

The village of Monte Sangrati was a wonderful place. It was cozy, hidden by the wooded mountains of central Italy. Its people were shepherds, farmers, and woodcutters. Their homes looked like dollhouses against the giant hills. Little shrines stood here and there along the hilly roads. Here, in 1218, a little girl was born. Her name was Zita.

When she was very young her mother told her about their rich, good Friend, who had put the mountains there long ago. And how He had filled them with trees and berries, furry animals, sweet water, and wild honey. She said He had done all this because He loved people. The name of that Friend was God.

At night, when Zita had finished her bowl of goat's milk, her mother told her another story about this Friend. How up above the sky there was a world that never ended. A place where there was no tiredness, and never any tears. This was God's home, called Heaven. He had invited everyone to come and live with Him. And to get there all anyone had to do was to love Him enough to do the little that He asked of them on earth. The secret, her mother said, was for Zita to learn to love Him a little bit more than she loved herself. Then keeping His rules would make her happy.

Zita loved Him. She thanked Him for the fun of play and the green-feel of the woods. She thanked Him every time her sturdy teeth chewed bread. She thanked Him for the warm, rough walls of home, for the puddles she paddled in, and the caves He had made for hide-and-seek. It was so easy to love Him!

One night Zita's parents told her they could not keep her with them any longer. She was twelve years old and her family were very poor. They told her they had found work for her in the city of Lucca, ten miles away. She would be a servant in the home of Pagano di Fatinelli, a rich weaver of wool and silk. She would leave them, her mother said sadly, but her Friend would always be with her.

[160]

In Lucca everything was strange to Zita. The other servants did not like her. They made fun of her for getting up to pray in the middle of the night and for giving her food to beggars. They thought she was unfriendly because she did not gossip with them or swear. They complained to the di Fatinellis about her.

Zita was lonely and homesick and afraid of losing her job. She worked harder and prayed harder to the Friend who had always been kind to her. Soon the di Fatinellis realized what a fine servant they had in this busy little country girl. They made her their head housekeeper.

In those days the rich always gave a little plain food to beggars. Zita was in charge of this giving. Pagano di Fatinelli decided one day to check over his supply of beans. Zita was frightened, for she had given most of them to the poor. She told his wife what she had done. Together, the women led the master to the storage bins. But the beans were all there! The measures were running over! Zita's rich Friend, God, had shown His generosity by replacing more beans than she had given to His poor!

Then there was the Christmas Eve when a terrible storm lashed Lucca. Zita was dressing for church. If she was foolish enough to go out in this storm, her master said, then she must wear his fine fur coat to keep her warm. Leaving the church, Zita saw a pitiful beggar at the door. He was blue with cold. Without thinking, she threw the coat over him and ran home. At the door she remembered it was her master's fur coat, and not her own cloth one, she had given away! She tried to explain, and he tried to understand. But the loss was a serious one, and he was very angry. Zita asked God to help her.

Hours later, as the family was about to sit down to their Christmas feast, a well-dressed stranger appeared at the door. He handed the fur coat over his arm to Zita. The whole family tried to thank him, to offer him wine and food. But he disappeared as quickly as he had come. Ever since that day, the door of the church of San Frediano in Lucca, where Zita met the beggar, has been called, "The Angel Door."

Saint Zita died in her master's house on April 27, 1278. She was sixty years old. She had learned how to love her Friend, God, even more than she loved herself.

SAINT ANTHONY OF PADUA

THE WONDER-WORKER

The Adriatic Sea separates the peninsula of Italy from Yugoslavia, Albania, and Greece. It is a beautiful sea, long and wide, deep and dangerous.

On the Italian side of the Adriatic is the town of Rimini. In the year 1227 it was filled with quarrelsome, unhappy people. A gentle Franciscan monk, very much in love with Jesus, went to visit them. He thought that if they only knew about Jesus they would want to be like Him. He would tell them. Then they would change their ways and begin to love one another. He called them to him in the public square. He told them how they could live happily on earth for a lifetime. And then happily in Heaven, forever. All they had to do was to love Jesus enough to follow His teachings. He expected them to listen. But they laughed at him, yawned, and turned away. They told him to get out of town, and the quicker the better.

The gentle monk was surprised and heartbroken. It was his first sermon to strangers. He had failed. Bitterly disappointed, he left town and walked along the seashore, blaming himself. A few idlers followed him, throwing sticks and calling names. The little monk felt worthless and ashamed. How disappointed Jesus must be with him, he thought. He was no preacher, no teacher at all. But what a surprise was in store for them. This is the way the story has come down to us:

The gentle monk looked out over the Adriatic Sea, sparkling in the sunshine. Men wouldn't listen to him. Probably fishes wouldn't either. Poor little fishes, he thought. No one has ever bothered to tell them about Jesus. Maybe he was good enough for that. He called to them: "Will you listen to me, little fishes?"

Down in the dark watery world there was a stir. All that fishes had ever known from man before were hooks and nets and death. The water heaved, and a message ran through it, calling them all to the shore.

The little silvery minnows came first and lined up at the water's edge. Behind them were all the fishes of the sea. They arranged themselves in perfect order, according to size and kind. Far out, past the dolphins and the sharks, were the great humps of whales. The wild Adriatic calmed, its only movement now were gentle wavelets filling the pulsing gills of the fishes.

Filled with joy, the little monk leaned toward them. He told them how much Jesus loved them. How He had given them the boundless sea for food and shelter. How He had made the sun to warm them, the night to rest them, the moonlight to guide them, the wind to stir and sweep their watery home. The listening fishes bowed their heads when he had finished. He blessed them and they swam away.

We are told that turning from the sea, he saw the people who had followed him. They were on their knees, marveling at what they had seen. He was not angry with them. They were his brothers. Humbly he told them Jesus had made up for his poor preaching with a miracle.

The gentle monk was Saint Anthony of Padua. He was soon to catch

more than fishes with his beautiful sermons. He was to become every-one's saint, loved by all races and creeds.

Anthony was born a noble, in a castle in Lisbon, Portugal, five or ten years before the opening of the thirteenth century. He was christened Fernando de Bulhões. His father was Treasurer to the King of Portugal. Not until he became a Franciscan monk was he given the name, Anthony. He came to Italy, and spent the last years of his life in Padua. There, thieves came to him with their stolen goods, and were persuaded to return them to their rightful owners. This is probably how he became the patron of lost articles. Through him, enemies found friendship again and unbelievers found faith.

Saint Anthony died in Italy on June 13, 1231. He was canonized the following year.

And yet it seems as if Saint Anthony never died. A thousand times a day, all over the world, people call to him as if he were just in the next room:

> *"Saint Anthony, please come around,*
> *Something's lost that can't be found!"*

And the happy friend of all of us comes running and laughing down the centuries, glad that we've called him. And suddenly we know where to look for that lost mitten or money or ring, for that vanished love or faith.

SAINT ELIZABETH

QUEEN OF HUNGARY

Today, Thuringia is part of central, industrial Germany. Only the toy makers and the dark Thuringian Forest remain to tell you how enchanting this country was in the thirteenth century.

Although its rulers have changed, the toy makers remain. Their art has been handed down from father to son for hundreds of years. Their wonderful wind-ups; dancing dolls and elves; feathered, mechanical birds that sing; jumping jacks; and the prettiest Christmas tree ornaments, still delight hearts that never grow old, as once they delighted Saint Elizabeth of Hungary.

In the thirteenth century this was a land of high, heavily wooded hills and tall, ancient trees, of wayside shrines and giant mushrooms, of laughing streams and secret waterfalls. Woodcutters, hermits, and gypsies lived in the woods. Robbers and pirates hid in them. Wild boar, speckled deer, and hare fled before the sound of the huntsman's horn. The villages were in the valleys; towns grew around the monasteries; the tall battlements of nobles' castles were lost in the mountain mists. During its happiest time this enchanted land was ruled by a young Landgrave, or Chief Count, Louis IV of Thuringia and his wife, Elizabeth.

Elizabeth was only fourteen years old when she married Louis. She was born in 1207 in Bratislava, the capital of Old Hungary, to King András II and his queen. Her parents were strong supporters of the church, and the little Princess Elizabeth was reared in a Christian world. It was the only world she ever wanted to know.

Elizabeth and her husband were very happy. They were young and they loved each other dearly. Their happiness spread over their land like a blessing. With Christ-like sweetness they cared for the poor, the sick, and the old. Three lovely children were born to them, and their life in this forest land was lovely as a fairy tale.

Louis IV of Thuringia was a brave, strong Christian and one day, along with his knights, he went off on a crusade. Proudly, Elizabeth and her children watched him ride away until his shining armor was only a twinkle in the dusty distance. Fondly she hoped, along with all of Christian Europe, that the knights of this crusade would be victorious, and gain the Holy Land from the infidels who held it.

For months, Elizabeth prayed, cared for her children, and performed the gentle works of love that had endeared her not only to her husband and his countrymen, but to God. She missed Louis. She prayed constantly for his safety. But she never tried to bring him back from this dangerous task. For this crusade was an act of love for Jesus, whom they both adored.

In 1227 word reached Elizabeth that Louis had been killed at Otranto. Her darling husband was dead. They would not meet again until they met in Heaven. In sorrow Elizabeth cried: "The world is dead to me, and all that was joyous in the world!"

And from that moment, her happy world was dead. God in His heaven and Louis were all she longed for, now. She put aside her lovely dresses and her costly jewels, and put on the dark brown, scratchy woolen robe of the Third Order of Saint Francis. Looking like a beggar, she placed herself under a stern director. She cared more tenderly and more tirelessly than ever for the poor, the sick, and the aged.

For four years Elizabeth suffered harsh treatment from her superior with great humility, and in those years of darkness and loneliness, her love for God, like a lamp growing brighter and brighter, led her into heroic self-sacrifice.

Like a little, worn beggar woman, Elizabeth died in 1231. She was just twenty-four years old. But she had pressed into that short life centuries of loving and giving. She had taken God's gifts with joy and shared them, she had carried the Cross He gave her with unfailing love. She was canonized Saint Elizabeth of Hungary in 1235, just four years after her death.

SAINT BRIDGET

PATRON OF SWEDEN

Bridget, or Birgitta, was born about 1303. She was the daughter of
Birger Persson, governor of Uppland, Sweden, and his wife, Ingeborg.
Bridget's mother died when she was twelve years old, and she was sent
to live with an aunt at Aspenäs on the lovely Lake Sommen. In her
teens Bridget married a wealthy young landowner, Ulf Gudmarsson,
and moved to his estate at Ulfasa. There she lived the life of a feudal
lady, and there eight children were born to her.

In 1335 Bridget was made lady in waiting to the Swedish Queen, Blanche. She soon discovered that the King, Magnus II, was weak and wicked, and the queen, far too lazy and luxury-loving. She did her best to arouse them to the needs of their people. Though they loved her, they left her advice unheeded. Trouble seemed to follow Bridget in these years. Her eldest daughter made a disgraceful marriage, and her youngest son, Gudmar, died. Filled with sorrow, Bridget asked to leave the court, and she and Ulf went on a Christian pilgrimage together. On their return to Sweden Ulf fell ill and was anointed for death. Bridget prayed while she cared for him, and he recovered. Both vowed, at the sign of this favor from Heaven, to devote the rest of their lives to God. Ulf entered a monastery at Alvastra, Sweden, and died there in 1344. Bridget remained in Alvastra as a penitent for four years, devoting herself to prayer, the care of the sick and poor. She continued to be troubled about her country's rulers, and again she warned the Swedish king and queen to mend their ways. For a time Magnus tried to improve his rule, and it was then that he made provision for the monastery Bridget built at Vadstena. Here she established her order of Bridgettine nuns. Well into the fifteenth century this monastery was the literary center of Sweden.

Now Magnus sought to have Bridget agree to an expedition he wished to make against the weak Letts and Estonians. She knew this was no crusade of love, but a plundering force designed to rob smaller countries. She opposed him, scolded him, told him his plan was evil, and that he could not deceive her. Magnus became very angry, and Bridget was no longer welcome at the court. But she still went traveling through the country, looking after the spiritual and worldly welfare of her people. The Christian faith was new to many of them. Her visits strengthened their bodies and their souls. If her presence embarrassed the king, it was beloved among the people, and while she was with them their faith burned bright.

In 1349 Bridget visited Italy. Here her faith and devotion revived the weakened spirits of the Christian Romans. They needed Bridget's example and zeal then, for their churches were falling apart. Their leader, the pope, was in exile at Avignon in France, and they felt abandoned. From Rome she went to Bologna, preaching against evil in high places by word and by deed, and in low places offering help and motherly love. In Bologna, she was joined by her daughter Catherine, who later also became a saint. For years Bridget had longed to visit the Holy Land. Now she gathered her children together and with Catherine and her sons Charles and Birger and other companions set off on a long pilgrimage. Charles, her favorite son, died in her arms on the way.

On this pilgrimage, it is said, Bridget had dreams or visions in which she saw the famous places in the Holy Land as they were in the time of Christ. She seems to have been filled with sorrow for the world and with warnings of things to come. For she hastened to Cyprus and boldly told the rulers there to repent or suffer the judgment of God. In Naples, later, her warnings were read from the pulpit by the priests. Weakened and old, she returned to Rome in March 1373, and there on July 23, she died. Her body was carried in a great procession through Dalmatia, Austria, Poland, and Danzig to Vadstena, where she was laid to rest in the monastery she had founded to spread the love of God and of learning among her people. Bridget was canonized in 1391.

SAINT CATHERINE OF SIENA

PATRON OF ITALY

Saint Catherine was born on March 25, 1347, to Giacomo and Lapa Benincasa in Siena, Italy. She was next to the youngest of twenty-five children. Her father was a skillful dyer and tanner, and there was much demand for his leatherwork.

Giacomo's busy shop was attached to his house. Through the rooms each day poured talk of family, workmen, customers, salesmen, relatives, and friends. Listening, little Catherine early became acquainted with the news, gossip, and habits of the world. She learned that wars and sickness and a weakening faith troubled Italy, and that the pope was no longer in Rome, which was his real home. The French held him a prisoner in a palace at Avignon.

But in the evenings, in the firelight of the great Benincasa kitchen, with the family gathered around, she heard other stories of a different world as her father and mother read aloud the lives of the saints and hermits. These romantic adventures aroused her imagination, and very early in her life she fell in love with the Jesus who inspired her heroes.

She fell so deeply and completely in love with Him that she made a secret vow never to marry, to give her heart, her body, her mind and soul to Him alone, forever, and to pattern her life after his.

Catherine was a gay, pretty little girl cherished by her family and popular with her playmates. When she told her friends the stories of the saints and their adventures, she made her tales so exciting that the children begged for more. And when she told them about Jesus, she made Him seem far more fascinating than any king or prince or knight who ever lived.

Catherine was trained at home to become a wife and mother. When she was old enough to marry, she disappointed her parents by telling them she had already promised herself to Jesus, whom she must serve with all of herself, all of her life. Her parents thought she was being stubborn or shy or foolish. They punished her severely, and made her a servant in her home. They thought this would soon change her mind and she would do as they wished. But Catherine did not object to the long hours of drudgery. She did her work well and offered her disgrace to Jesus, as a little gift. While her hands performed the tiresome chores, her heart was talking to Him whom she loved most of all. Sometimes, when she felt especially close to Him, He seemed to come to her in visions to comfort her.

Catherine suffered much for her beloved Jesus. She wished to become a Dominican nun, and her family refused their permission. Then, worn out with longing, she fell ill and came close to death. Frightened, her mother promised that if she recovered, she could enter the Dominican order. Catherine regained her health very soon.

Now, as a nun, she began to care for the poor and sick with great love and tenderness. She devoted herself to the most neglected and unpleasant ones, and those with the most repulsive diseases. Miracles of healing were now attributed to her, and her fame began to spread all over Italy.

Many considered Catherine a saint. Others thought her simply clever or full of tricks. The pope, hearing these different stories, summoned her to be questioned by doctors of the church. After these wise men had talked to her, they too were convinced of her holiness and became her followers.

Now nobles, warriors, and rulers sought her advice and prayers. So highly was she esteemed that she was now asked to perform an almost impossible feat: to bring the pope back to Rome from his luxurious palace-prison in Avignon!

Catherine begged God to help her. She prayed that, if He wanted the pope back in Rome, He would give her the wisdom and courage to perform this great task. Then she went to visit the holy father in France. When she was with him she told him how weak the faith in Italy had become without his strong hand to guide it, how lonely Rome was without him in it. Listening to her, he agreed to return! But first she must get permission from the French king, for he was his prisoner.

The king and the cardinals were so impressed by this brilliant nun's argument and holiness that they agreed, and soon the pope began the dangerous journey back to Rome.

Catherine did all this at a time of the world when women, especially peasant women, had almost nothing to do with world affairs.

Now her health began to fail. Prayers, penances, and care of others had left her tired and she became seriously ill. She longed more than ever to be with her beloved Jesus.

Catherine of Siena died in her convent in Rome in 1380. She was thirty-three years old, the same age as Jesus, when He died.

SAINT SERGIUS

A RUSSIAN SAINT

A son called Bartholomew was born to a noble family near Rostov on the River Don in Russia in the year 1315.

Beyond Rostov, the Caucasus Mountain range begins: dark, thickly wooded, and mysterious. As a boy Bartholomew must have explored those mountains often on foot and found contentment in their loneliness, for by the time he was twenty he went with his brother Stephen to live as a *pustiniky,* or man of the wilderness, in the deep woods beyond Moscow. Here they built rough huts and a chapel. Here, from a visiting abbot, Bartholomew took monastic vows and was given the name, Sergius. Because he was not yet ordained, a priest from Kiev dedicated the three little buildings in the woods to the Most Holy Trinity. Shortly after this, Stephen left his brother to join a monastery in Moscow. For many years Sergius lived alone. Removed from the world, he hoped to discover what God wished him to do with his life.

Sergius had to fight the same temptations that come to all of us. And in addition he had physical enemies to endure. Ice, snow, wind and rain and bitter cold lashed him through the long Russian winters. But he had friends in this wilderness, too: fire and light and the wild bears he tamed.

One by one, curious and troubled people found his hiding place. Very soon he had many followers. The more who came to him, the more vividly he knew that God wished him to minister to them, to become a priest, and get busy about God's work on earth.

A tall young lad had gone into the wilderness. A powerful, bearded man, sparing of speech and gesture, came out.

Sergius studied and was ordained a priest at Pereyaslav Zalesky, near Moscow. Then he returned to the woods, enlarged the monastery of the Holy Trinity, and opened it to monks under the rule of Saint Benedict. Hundreds of disciples flocked to him and the peace around him. The forest was cleared, a village grew up, a road was beaten into it by the footsteps of his followers. Sergius's warmth and understanding of people drew many souls to God, from among all walks of life.

Prince Dmitry Donskoy sought his prayers and advice before his great victory over the Tartars at Kulikovo Polye in 1380, the battle which marked the beginning of the end of pagan Tartar power in Russia.

Saint Sergius is Russia's most outstanding saintly figure. Probably more than any other single man, he was able by his example to restore his people's self-respect and trust in God, in the face of bitter wars and oppression. He lived to be almost eighty years old, and died among his monks at the monastery of the Holy Trinity outside Moscow in 1392. In 1917 the monastery was forcibly closed by the Bolshevists and the saint's relics placed in a People's Museum. In 1945 permission was given to reopen the Monastery, and the beloved relics were restored.

SAINT JEANNE D'ARC

SAVIOR OF FRANCE

The bravest soldier who ever lived was a little French country girl who loved sewing and spinning and all womanly things. And her story is one of the strangest and saddest in the world. Her name was Jeanne d'Arc. She was born on January 6, 1412, in Domrémy, on the Meuse River, in the hill country of eastern France. Jeanne was the third of five children born to Jacques and Isabelle d'Arc. All those who knew Jeanne as a girl in Domrémy loved her, and her childhood was happy in spite of her country's troubles.

All the while Jeanne was growing up her country was at war with England. And at war with itself. France's two most powerful duchies, Burgundy and Orléans, were fighting with each other. By the time Jeanne was twelve years old, England had conquered most of France.

Jeanne had never seen an army. But she had heard about battles from wounded soldiers who dragged themselves into Domrémy for care and shelter from their enemies. Once her village was attacked, but the families fled before the army arrived. They returned, to find their food gone, their fields burned, their church destroyed. The people of Domrémy worked hard to restore their homes and farms and church.

There were no schools in Domrémy, and Jeanne never learned to read and write. But the village priest taught the children much more than their prayers and catechism. He told them about Jesus and the saints. He gave them the history of France through tales of its heroes and its kings. They knew that Charles VII, called the Dauphin, was their rightful king. They knew that as long as he was uncrowned, France had no real leader. And so it was that at the little church in Domrémy, Jeanne learned to love God, her country, and her king.

One day, when Jeanne was working in her father's field, she saw a blinding flash of light. A voice she had never before heard called her. She saw no one, and was frightened. She was so frightened that she did not hear what the voice was saying to her. And she told no one. But a few days later she heard voices calling her again. She heard them many times, after that. They told her something she could not believe. That *she* was to save France! That *she* was to lead an army! That through *her* Charles VII would be crowned King of France at the cathedral in Rheims! She was fourteen years old when she understood what the voices were telling her. She answered them by saying that she could not ride a horse. She did not know how to use a sword. She could not read and write. She was a girl, and only men were warriors.

Her father was strict, and Jeanne kept this secret for two years because she was afraid that he would punish her if he heard it. Finally the voices told her that she must obey them. They said that God commanded her. Only then did she agree to do what was asked of her.

France was in grave danger, her voices said. She must go to Robert Baudringcourt, the commander of the king's forces, in the town of Vaucouleurs. She confided first in her uncle. He took her to Vaucouleurs. When Robert Baudringcourt saw her, he laughed. When he listened to her, he laughed louder. Turning to her uncle, he said: "Send the maiden home. She is off her head!"

Jeanne's uncle took her home. The voices told her to go back. When she returned, Robert Baudringcourt did not laugh. She had told him on her first visit of a great defeat the king's army would suffer. And the army had suffered this defeat. He arranged for her to see the Dauphin. He gave her an escort of three soldiers and her brother. Jeanne wore men's clothing for this trip.

Charles VII knew she was coming to see him at Chinon. He took off his crown and royal robes and put them on another. Simply dressed to disguise his royalty, he mingled with the crowd at court. But when Jeanne arrived she went straight toward him.

"I am not the king," he said, pointing to the man who wore the crown.

"Sire, you are the king," she answered, though she had never seen him before.

The king turned her over to a court to be examined. After three weeks of testimony they advised Charles to allow her to lead the army. On April 27, 1429, Jeanne led the army from Blois. Her standard bore the words "Jesus: Maria." On May 8, her army defeated the English at Orléans. She defeated them again at Patay. The English surrendered

at Troyes. The road to Rheims was cleared. On July 17, 1429, Charles VII was crowned King of France in Rheims!

Now Jeanne had completed her task. But the king would not allow her to return home. She continued to lead the army. Soon she was taken prisoner and John of Luxembourg sold her to the English. She went on trial at Rouen and was condemned to death. On Tuesday, May 29, 1431, Jeanne d'Arc was burned at the stake in the market place of Rouen. As the flames were lighted, she asked that a cross be held before her eyes. Gazing at it, she called only one name in that long, bright agony, the name of the One dearest to her heart: "Jesus!"

Jeanne d'Arc was not quite twenty years old. Weeping among those who saw her die was John Tressart, secretary to King Henry VI of England. He cried: "We are lost: we have burned a saint!"

Jeanne d'Arc, known to us as Joan of Arc, was canonized in 1920.

SAINT CASIMIR

PATRON OF POLAND AND LITHUANIA

Prince Casimir was born about 1458, in the days of Poland's greatness as a kingdom. He was the second son of King Casimir IV of Poland and his wife, Elizabeth of Austria.

All of the royal Casimirs had been good Christians, brave warriors, and fine statesmen. Under them Poland had grown from the Baltic almost to the Black Sea. Great universities and libraries encouraged learning among their people.

Casimir and his brothers, Ladislaus and John, had as their tutor the famous historian, Jan Dlugosz. Not only was he a canon of Cracow, but he was a man of extraordinary learning, as well. The young princes loved him and imitated him in many ways. Bright, sensitive Casimir loved him most of all.

Jan Dlugosz's holiness and his warm understanding of the nature of his pupils drew out the best in the boys. In young Casimir he saw a lad whose heart and mind from early childhood leaned more toward Christ and His mother than toward his royal world. The boy wore plain clothes when he could easily have worn fine ones. Under his shirt he hid a prickly haircloth vest. He avoided softness and the personal luxury that surrounded him. He slept on the ground and wakened in the night to pray. Secretly he sought out the poor and gave them all he had and all that he could get from his father and his brother Ladislaus, who had recently become the young King of Bohemia. Yet with all this, the young prince was an appealing boy. He radiated happiness. He was dearly loved by all who knew him for his quick thoughtfulness and his pleasing way with people.

So admired was Casimir that when he was only fifteen years old the Hungarian nobles, displeased with their own king, Mátyás Hóllós, asked the King of Poland to allow them to place Casimir on their throne! Casimir did not want to be a king. But his father ordered him to take an army and seize the crown of Hungary. Casimir obeyed, unwillingly. Never was a less ambitious boy sent on such an errand.

At the frontier, Mátyás of Hungary had assembled an army. Casimir's troops were deserting, because they had not been paid. This young prince did not believe in war. He thought it cruel and unChristian. He knew he was not a coward, and he cared nothing at all what people thought of him. He looked at his soldiers, and we can well imagine what he was thinking: they should all be at home, building the Kingdom of God on earth, not trying to tear it down. And he was leading them into battle.

He might have inspired them into glorious victory. Instead, he consulted his officers; they advised him to take the army home. Casimir also knew that the pope had asked his father not to fight this war. Casimir then ordered his men to turn around and march back home. There would be no war, no taking of the Hungarian crown, or any other, by him.

Imagine what King Mátyás thought when he saw the Polish troops going home without a battle!

When Casimir returned, his father and the court would not allow him to enter Cracow, the capital. They were very angry. They were ashamed of him. He had made mighty Poland the clown of the world! The king had Casimir imprisoned for three months in a castle at Dobzki.

The young prince did not live very long after this. He spent the last few years of his life as he had wished to spend all of it, quietly, humbly, in study and prayer. Only once did he show his royal quality as a ruler of men, when for a short time during an absence of his father he was viceroy of Poland. He died of consumption in his middle twenties, and was canonized Saint Casimir in the year 1521.

To his people, he was always the beloved one. And they call him to this day, "The Peacemaker."